EXTRA ORDINARY BANNERS

for ordinary times

George Collopy

Resource Publications, Inc.
San Jose, California

Editorial Director: Kenneth Guentert
Design: George Collopy
Managing Editor: Elizabeth J. Asborno
Mechanical Layout: Terri Ysseldyke-All
Cover production: Huey Lee

Library of Congress Catalog Card Number: 92-347

ISBN 0-89390-225-X

© 1992 Resource Publications, Inc.
All rights reserved.

For reprint permission, write:
Reprint Department
Resource Publications, Inc.
160 E. Virginia Street, #290
San Jose, CA 95112-5876

96 95 94 93 92 | 5 4 3 2 1

St. Ambrose is credited with comparing the Christian to the bee and its activity, and the church to a beehive.

Contents

Introduction ix
Various Arrangements xi

The Art
PART I: Christian symbolism from art
of the European Renaissance period. 1

   The Universe:
      Earth 3
      Sun and Moon 5
      Clouds 7
      Stars 9
      Rainbow 11
      Water 13
      Fire 15
      Garden 17
      Wings 19
      Bee and Honey 21

   The Old Testament:
      Noah 23
      Jonah 25
      Moses 27
      Solomon 29
      Joseph 31
      David 33
      Samson 35

   The Animal World:
      Bear 37
      Camel 39
      Lamb 41
      Lion 43
      Stag 45
      Snail 47
      Grasshopper 49
      Bee 51
      Butterfly 53
      Frog 55
      Birds 57
      Owl 59
      Rooster 61

Eagle	63
Dove	65
Stork	67
Fish	69
Cat	71
Dog	73
Phoenix	75
Dragon	77

The Plant World:

Fruit	79
Apple	81
Cherry	83
Orange	85
Strawberry	87
Grape	89
Pear	91
Rose	93
Daisy	95
Poppy	97
Carnation	99
Violet	101
Narcissus	103
Lily	105
Hyacinth	107
Wheat	109
Thistle	111
Bulrush	113
Ivy	115
Clover	117

The Body:

Head	119
Eye	121
Ear	123
Hair	125
Heart	127
Hand	129
Foot	131
Skull	133
Stigmata	135

PART II: Christian symbolism from the quilt designs of the Early American period. 137

The Universe:
    Search the Bible 139
    Sunshine 141
    Sunlight and Darkness 143
    Sunshine and Shadow 145
    Star 147

The Old Testament:
    Garden of Eden 149
    Tree of Life 151
    Children of Israel 153
    Jacob's Ladder 155
    David and Goliath 157
    Job's Tears 159
    Job's Troubles 161
    Joseph's Coat 163
    Bear's Claws 165
    Which Way? 167

The Animal World:
    Birds 169
    Honey Bee 171
    Butterfly 173
    Snail's Trail 175
    Dove 177

The Plant World:
    Lily 179
    Rose 181
    Grapes 183
    Hearts and Flowers 185

The Body:
    Next-Door Neighbor 187
    Hands to Work, Hearts to God 189
    Peace and Plenty 191

The New Testament:
    Star of Bethlehem 193
    Christmas Star 195
    Carpenter's Square 197

Diamond and Square	199
Tree of Temptation	201
Grape Basket	203
Hosanna	205
King's Crown	207
Caesar's Crown	209
Crown of Thorns	211
Crown and Cross	213
Cross and Crown	215
Roman Cross	217
Crowned Cross	219
Starry Crown	221
Steps to the Altar	223
The Seven Upward Steps	225

Bibliography 227

Introduction

Extraordinary Banners is designed as a companion piece to *It's a Banner Year!* Whereas the latter concentrated on the major liturgical seasons, this new idea book presents over one hundred different banner designs for use mainly during ordinary times.

Many of the banners are based on examples of religious symbolism found in the art of the European Renaissance period. Brief notes explaining the origins are included.

New to this field is a large selection of banners based on designs from Early American quilts. It has been generally agreed that quilts are pieces of art in their own right, but what is not recognized is that these quilts have a definite religious basis. Art and religion were a part of everyone's daily life in this period, and reading the Bible provided inspiration for virtually all of the quilt projects.

No attempt has been made to provide instructions on the mechanical side of banner preparation. There are many excellent books on the subject listed in the bibliography. Refer to these for new approaches. Use the following designs only as a point of departure. Copy them "as is," dissect them, abstract them, combine them with others, but in all cases have fun! I'm certain the final result will illuminate your own and your viewers' search for God.

To Start

Read the paperback on *Environment and Art in Catholic Worship.* It espouses the cause of the artist and states that the art consultant should be an integral member of the liturgy commission. It reaffirms that the "art *of our own days* coming from every race and region, shall be given free scope in the Church...." You can't find a better starting point.

To Enlarge

There are a number of ways to quickly and accurately enlarge the banner designs. For your convenience in reproducing the art, the pages have been perforated.

Reproductive stats, for preparing artwork for printing, are available at quick-print shops and are priced according to size.

Opaque projectors, available in all schools, will project flat artwork onto a vertical surface for retracing.

Overhead projectors will do the same as above, except that you will have to transfer your original piece of art to clear acetate before projecting.

Transposing with a grid system is another way to enlarge. Use the system of squares provided and draw the *same* number of grid squares in the enlarged size you want to reproduce. Working one square at a time, place a dot on each grid line of the enlarged pattern where the design is intersected on the small original pattern. Connect the dots.

To Color

A few suggestions have been made regarding color, but for the most part, you are on your own. It's always best to look at color swatches in the church itself, in both natural and artificial light. This enables you to judge the effect of the color and the light against the surroundings.

The traditional colors used in the church year are purple for Advent and Lent; white for Christmas and Easter, All Saints Day (November 1), John the Baptist (June 24), John the Evangelist (December 27), the Chair of Peter (February 22) and the Conversion of Paul (January 25), and for the feasts of the Lord (other than the Passion) and the feasts of Mary and the saints (other than the martyrs); red for Palm Sunday, Good Friday, Pentecost, celebrations of the Passion, birthdays of the apostles and evangelists, and for feasts of martyrs; green is normally used for ordinary time.

However, color restrictions are not as stringent today, and I would suggest reaching out for new combinations. See Jim Stockton's *Designer's Guide to Color* for ideas. This series has three wonderful paperbacks on color combinations. Also, study the paintings of our modern masters for exciting colors to adapt to your projects. Look to Matisse, Gauguin, Picasso, Stuart Davis, and Joan Miró. Investigate the innovative uses of color in the folk art of the Native American, the Eskimo, the Latin American, and, of course, the Amish.

Various Arrangements

All of the following banners have been designed for a square format. If this does not suit your particular need, consider the variations below. Also consult additional arrangements shown in the previous paperback, *It's a Banner Year!*

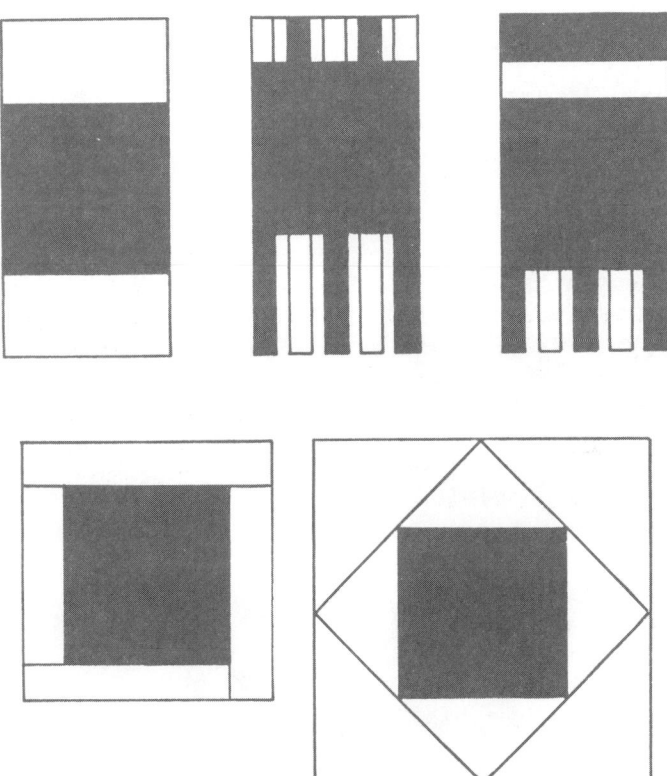

xi

PART I
Christian symbolism from art of the European Renaissance period.

A recent pontiff remarked that the Church's fundamental function is to direct humanity's gaze to the mystery of the Creator. The Church was the principal sponsor of the arts during the Renaissance period. And nowhere since that time has a sponsorship produced such a huge body of work that has helped direct the Christian's journey. In the Renaissance artist's search for God, he used many signs and symbols to illustrate the subject matter. Many of these seem obscure to us today, but to the people of the time they were a familiar sight, rooted in the teachings of the Bible and in the legends passed on from previous generations. Perhaps we, too, can learn from these symbols and signs to illuminate our journey.

The Universe:
Earth

The earth symbolizes the Church sheltering people and feeding them with spiritual faith.

The Universe:
Sun and Moon

The sun is a symbol of Christ. The moon represents the Virgin: Mary clothed with the sun and with the moon under her feet (Revelation 12:1).

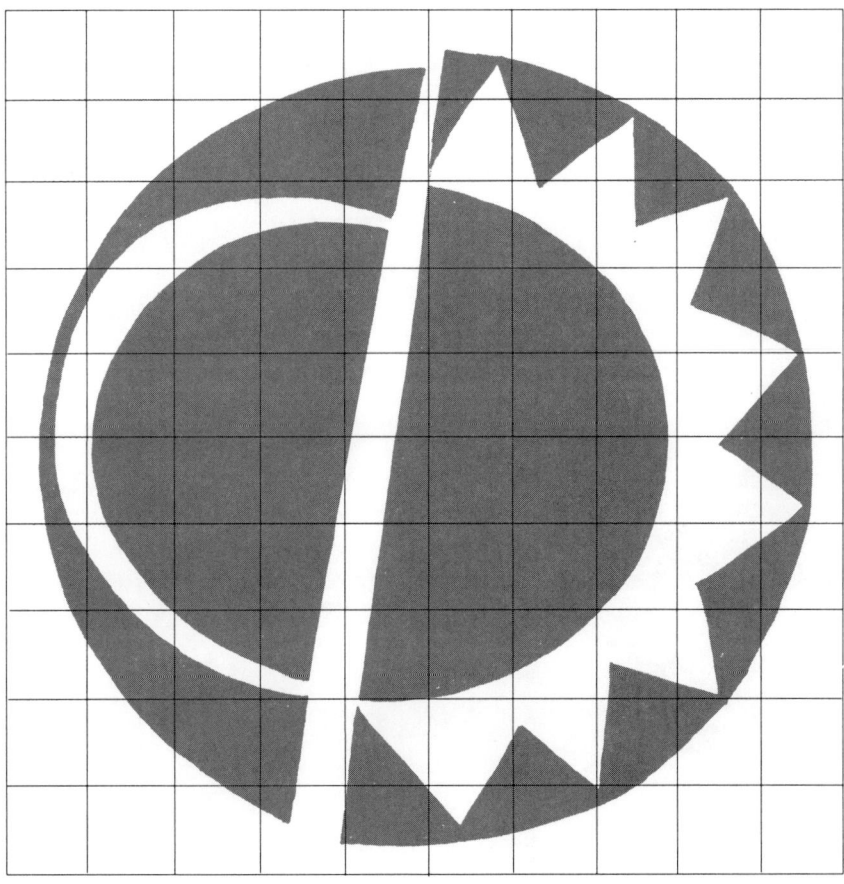

The Universe:
Clouds

Clouds obscuring the sky are a symbol of the unseen God.

The Universe:
Stars

The star is a symbol of divine guidance: the star of the East guiding the Magi. Twelve stars represent the twelve tribes of Israel. Mary's crown has twelve stars (Revelation 12:1).

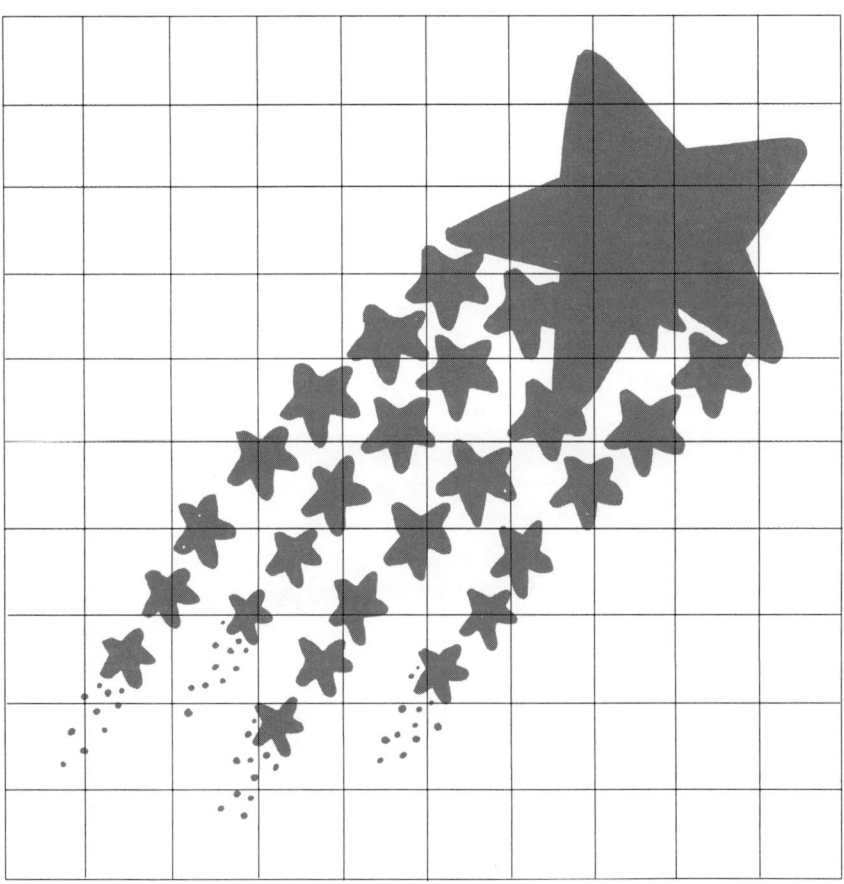

The Universe:
Rainbow

...and there was a rainbow round the throne" (Revelation 4:2,3).

The Universe:
Water

Water cleanses and purifies as in the sacrament of baptism.

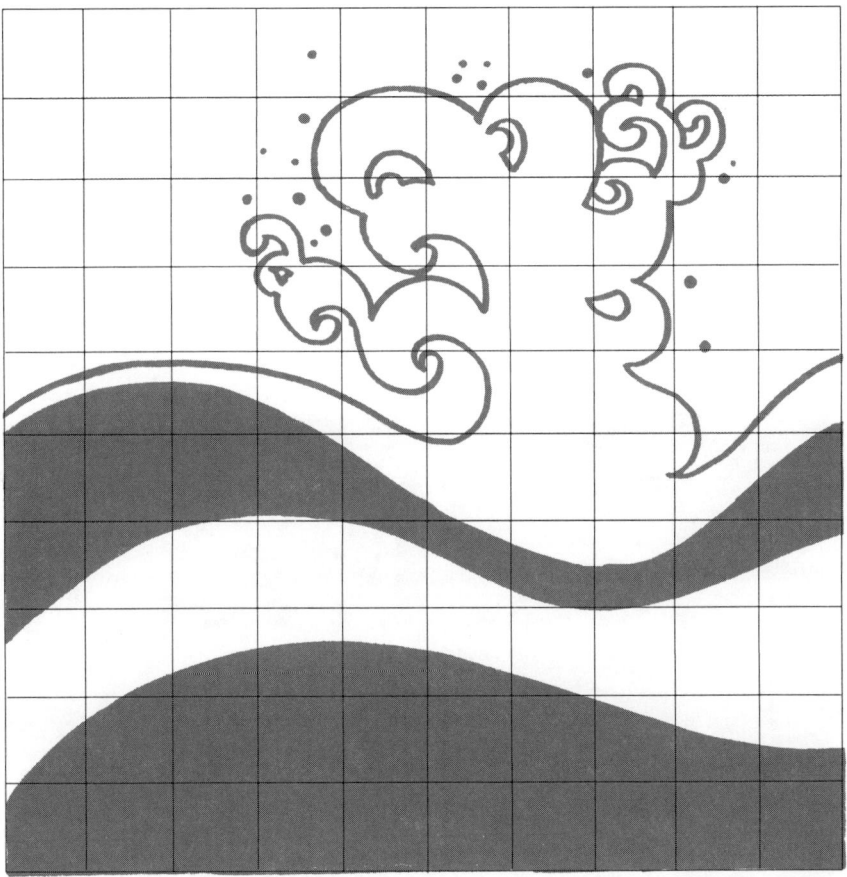

The Universe:
Fire

In addition to the torments of hell, fire and flames symbolize martyrdom and religious fervor.

The Universe:
Garden

A garden enclosed is a symbol of the Immaculate Conception.

The Universe:
Wings

Wings are the symbol of Divine Mission.

The Universe:
Bee and Honey

The bee symbolizes the Christian. Paradise is the land of milk and honey.

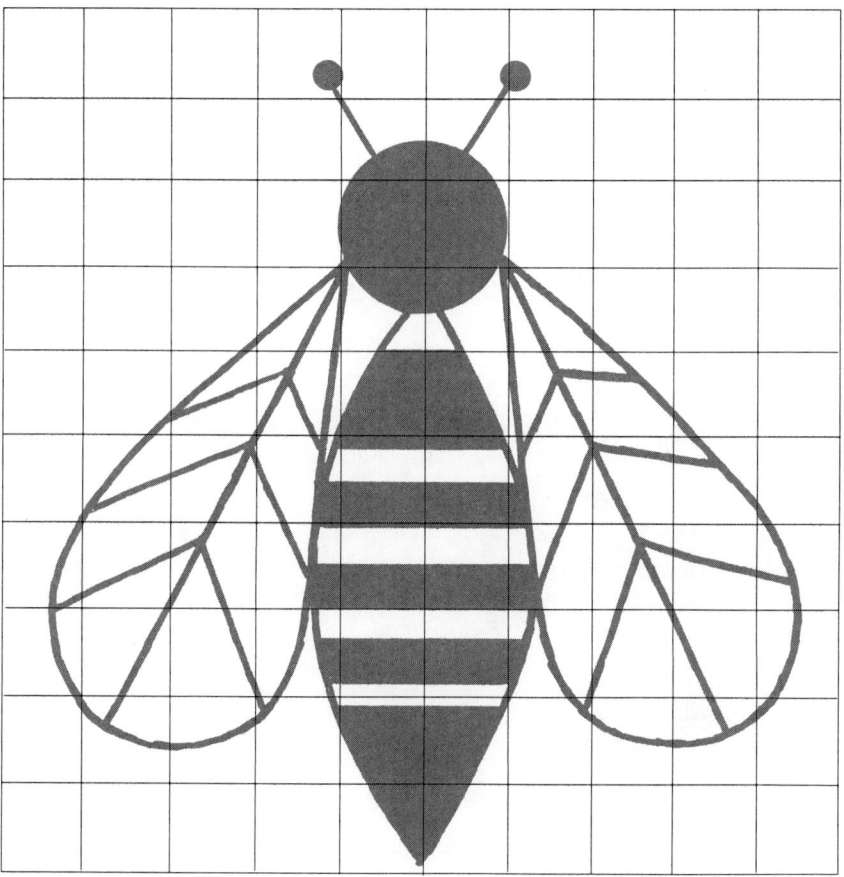

The Old Testament:
Noah

...and the Ark (Genesis 6:18,19).

The Old Testament:
Jonah

...and the whale (Jonah 1:17).

The Old Testament:
Moses

...and the burning bush (Exodus 3:2).

The Old Testament:
Solomon

...divide the living child in two (1 Kings 3:25).

The Old Testament:
Joseph

...and his coat of many colors (Genesis 37).

The Old Testament:
David
...played on his harp (1 Samuel 16:23).

The Old Testament:
Samson

...and Delilah (Judges 16:19).

The Animal World:
Bear

A symbol of Christianity. It was believed that bear cubs, born shapeless, were formed by the mother just as heathens are reformed by Christianity.

The Animal World:
Camel

A symbol of temperance, probably derived from the fact that camels can survive without drinking for long periods of time.

The Animal World:
Lamb

Behold the Lamb of God (John 1:29).

The Animal World:
Lion

A symbol of the Resurrection. It was believed that lion cubs were born dead and came alive only after three days.

The Animal World:
Stag

Typifies piety and religious aspiration. As the stag pants after water, so panteth my soul after thee, O God (Psalm 42:1).

The Animal World:
Snail

A symbol of laziness and of the sinner, since it is born and feeds in the mud.

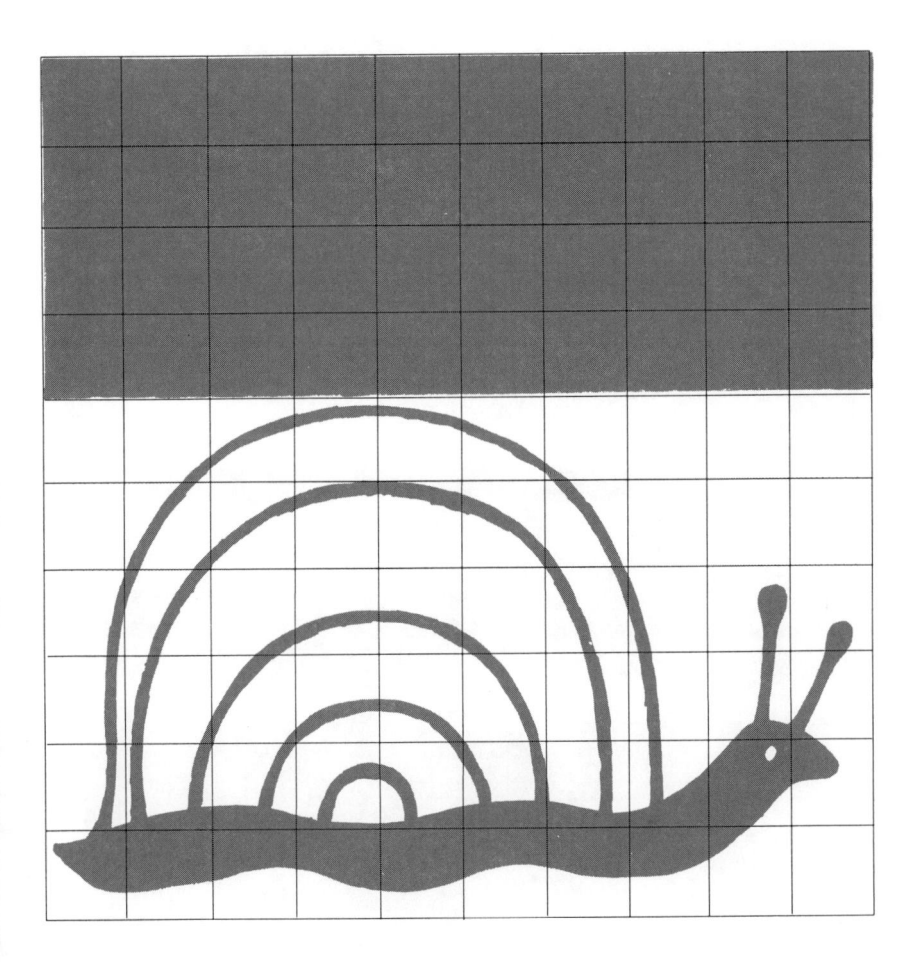

The Animal World:
Grasshopper

One of the plagues of Egypt, it has come to mean conversion to Christianity.

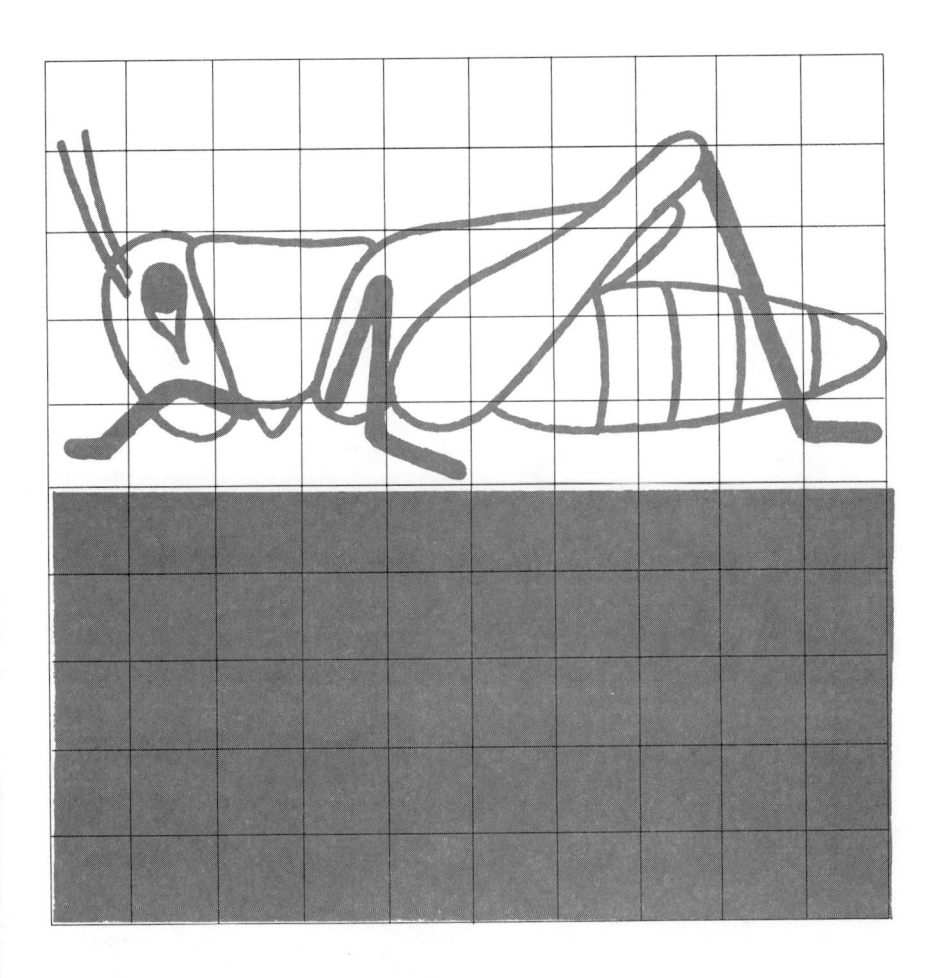

The Animal World:
Bee

St. Ambrose compared the church to a beehive and the Christian to a bee: industrious, sweet, and pious.

The Animal World:
Butterfly

A symbol of the Resurrection derived from its three stages of life: caterpillar, chrysalis, butterfly—life, death, resurrection.

The Animal World:
Frog

A symbol of hereticism, worldly pleasures, and sin. A rain of frogs was one of the plagues of Egypt (Exodus 8).

The Animal World:
Birds

Symbols of the winged soul or the spiritual life.

The Animal World:
Owl

Symbol of wisdom and an attribute of Christ. ...To give light to them that sit in darkness and in the shadow of death (Luke 1:79).

The Animal World:
Rooster

Associated with St. Peter, it expresses, denial and repentance (John 13:38).

The Animal World:
Eagle

Another symbol of the Resurrection (Isaiah 40:31). The eagle was thought to renew its youth by plunging into fire and then into water.

The Animal World:
Dove

A symbol of purity and peace, bringing the olive branch to Noah (Genesis 8).

The Animal World:
Stork

A symbol of prudence, piety, and chastity, the stork denotes the coming of spring, the Annunciation, the advent of Christ.

The Animal World:
Fish

A symbol of Christ, the five Greek letters forming the word "fish" are the first letters of the words "Jesus Christ God's Son Saviour."

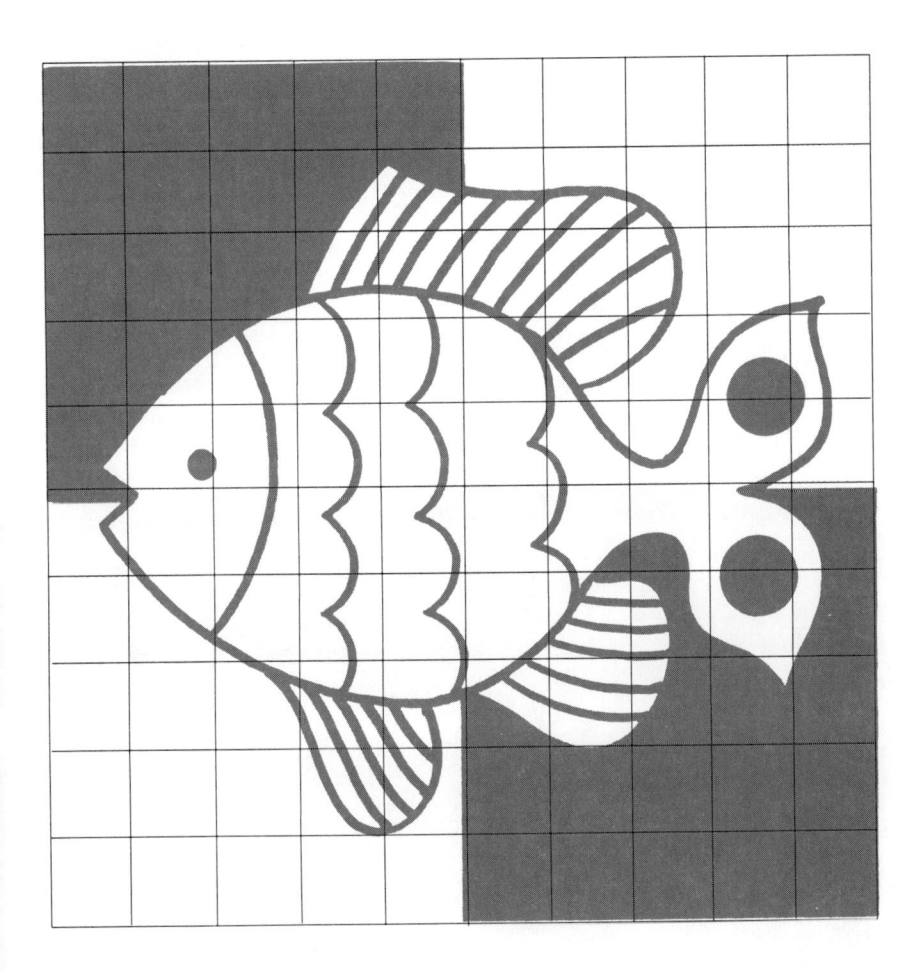

The Animal World:
Cat

At the birth of Christ, a cat gave birth to a litter of kittens in the stable. The cat is usually painted with a cross on its back.

The Animal World:
Dog

Ever faithful, such as the dog of St. Rock, who brought him food and waited at his side.

The Animal World:
Phoenix

Another symbol of the Resurrection, the phoenix periodically rises from its own funeral pyre and begins a new cycle of life.

The Animal World:
Dragon

The enemy of God (Revelation 12:7-9).

The Plant World:
Fruit

There are twelve fruits of the spirit: peace, joy, love, gentleness, goodness, long-suffering, patience, meekness, faith, modesty, temperance, and chastity.

The Plant World:
Apple

The Latin word for apple is the same as that for evil; hence, the allusion to the forbidden fruit.

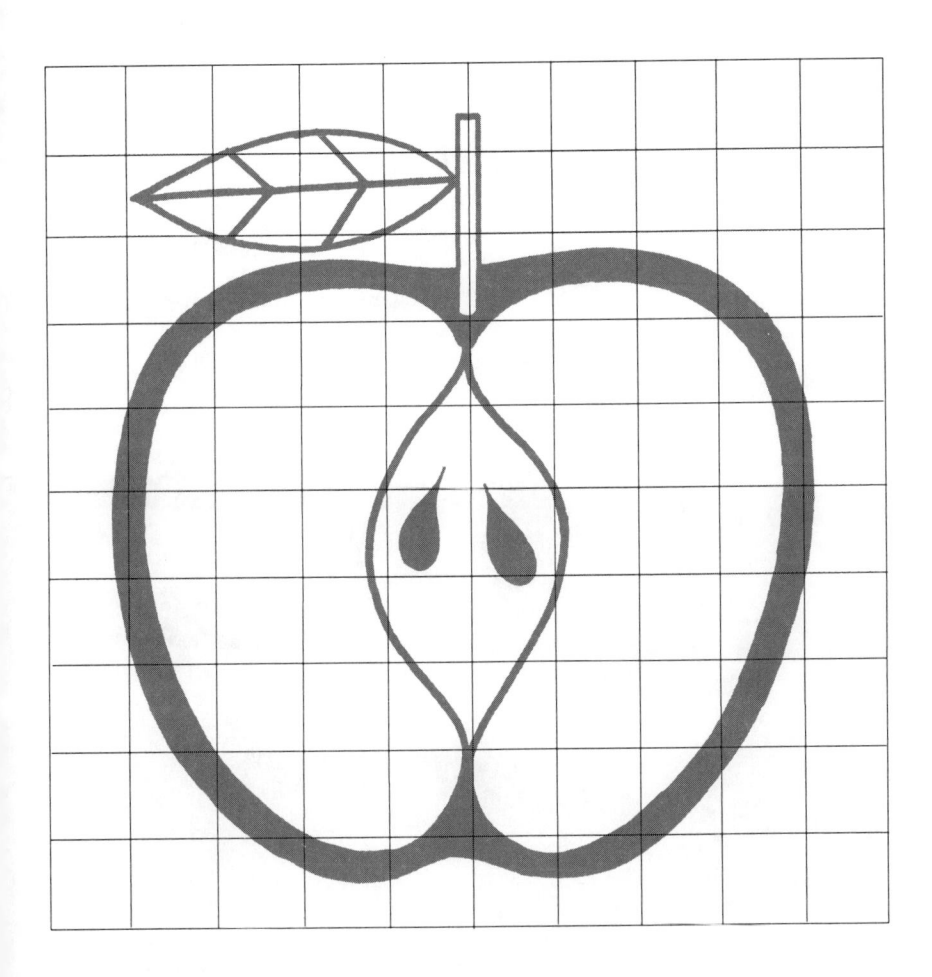

The Plant World:
Cherry

"The fruit of paradise" symbolizes the sweet character derived from good works.

The Plant World:
Orange
A symbol of generosity, chastity, and purity.

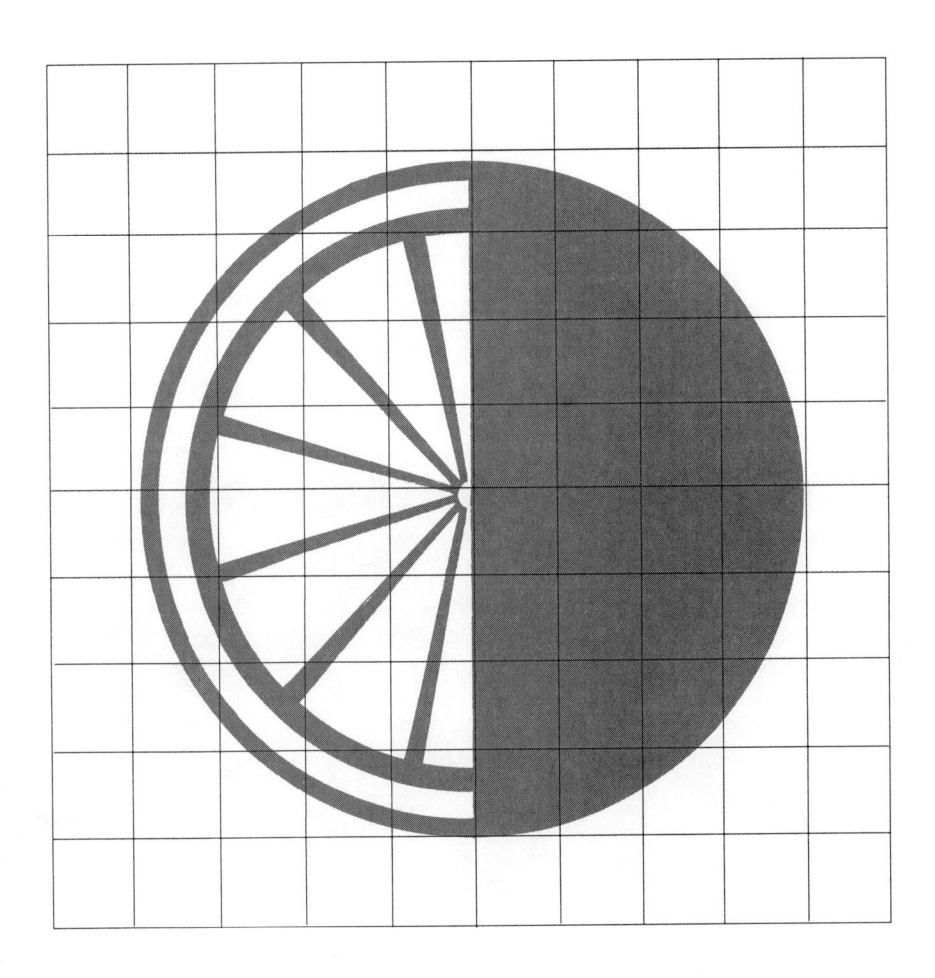

The Plant World:
Strawberry

A symbol of the good works of a righteous person.

The Plant World:
Grape

Like Eucharistic wine, the grape symbolizes the blood of Christ.

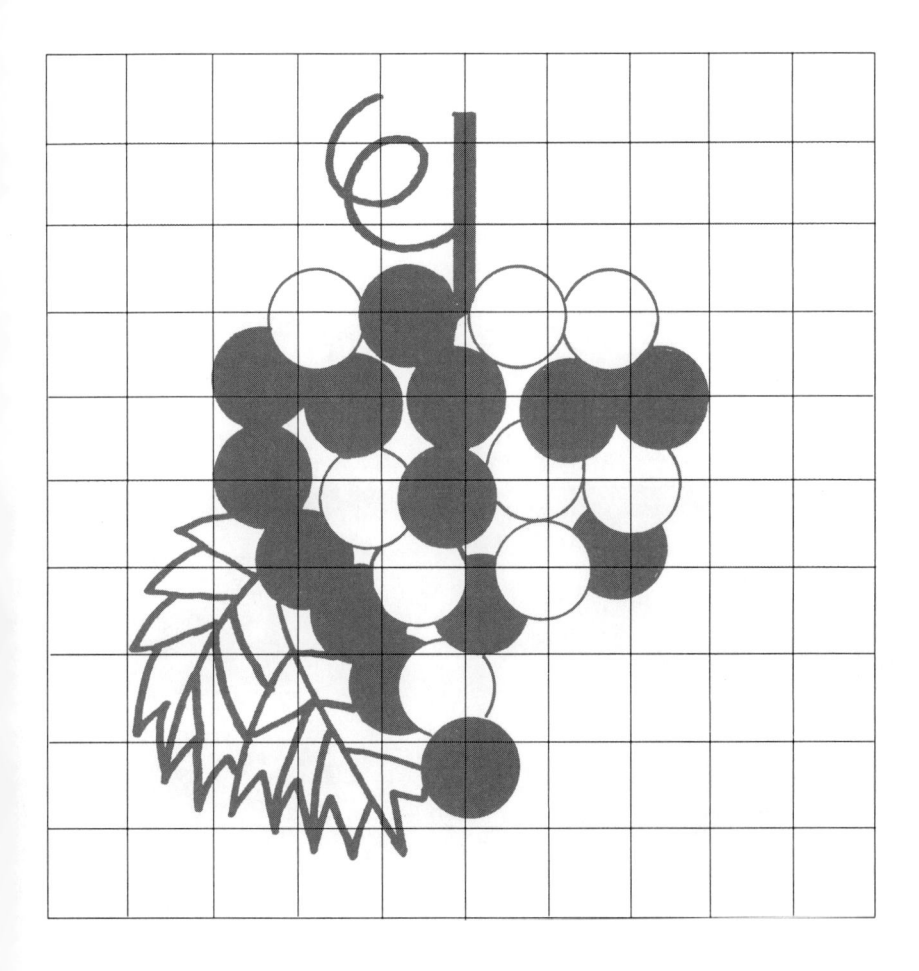

The Plant World:
Pear

Refers to Christ's love for humankind.

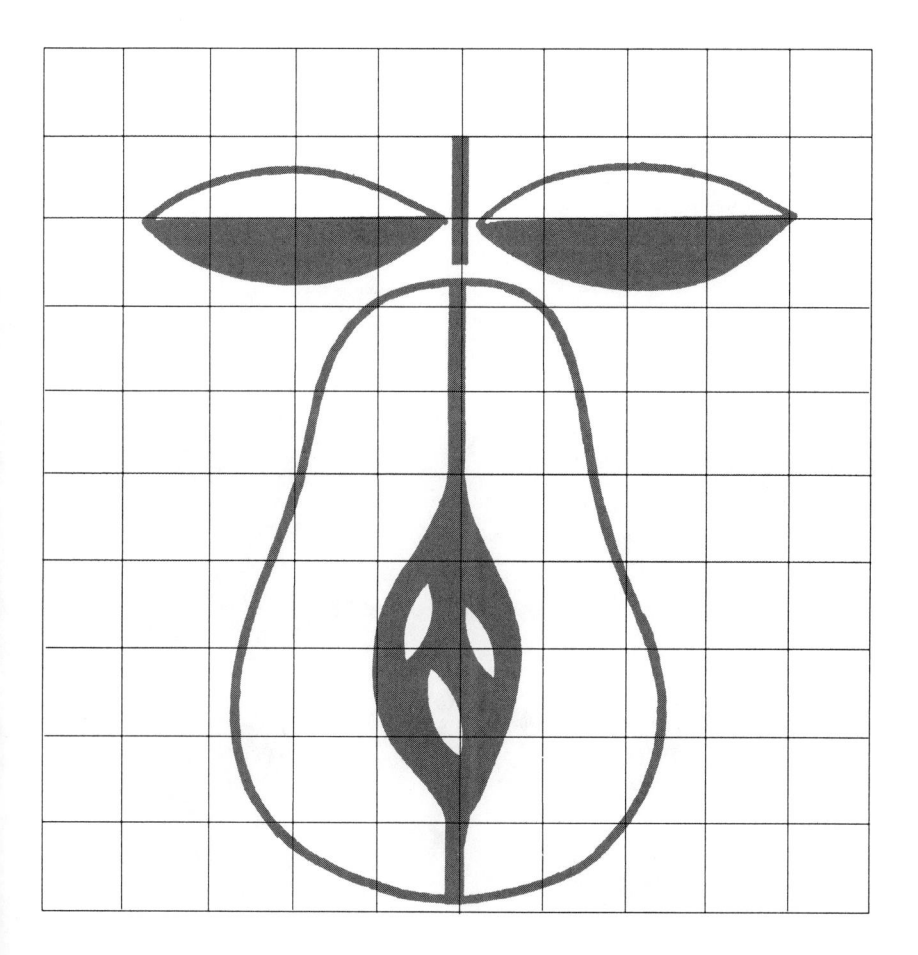

The Plant World:
Rose

A red rose is a symbol of martyrdom; the white rose, purity.

The Plant World:
Daisy
The innocence of the Christ child.

The Plant World:
Poppy

A symbol of sleep and death, alluding to the Passion of Christ.

The Plant World:
Carnation

The red carnation is a symbol of pure love; the pink carnation, marriage.

The Plant World:
Violet

A symbol of humility.

The Plant World:
Narcissus

A symbol of self-love and indifference, probably derived from the Greek legend.

The Plant World:
Lily

A symbol of purity.

The Plant World:
Hyacinth

Originally derived from pagan mythology, it has come to mean peace of mind and a desire for heaven.

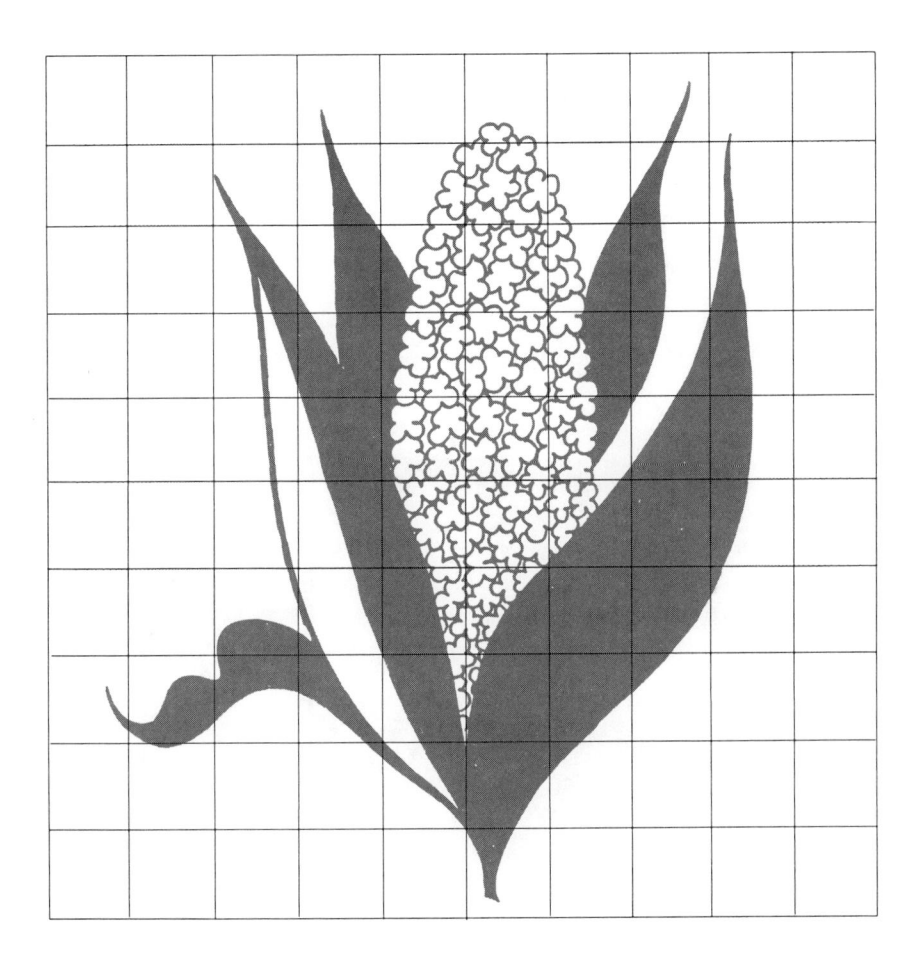

The Plant World:
Wheat
The bread of the Eucharist.

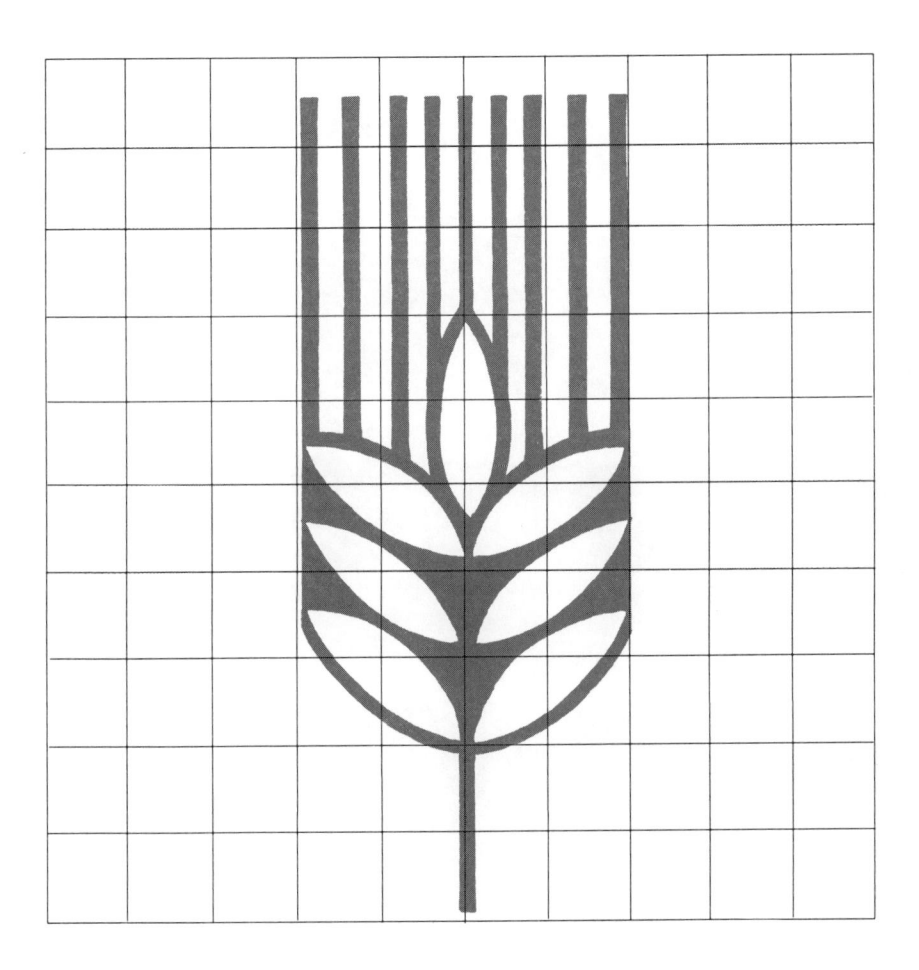

The Plant World:
Thistle

A symbol of earthly sorrow and sin.

The Plant World:
Bulrush

A symbol of the faithful who lead a humble life and obey the laws of God.

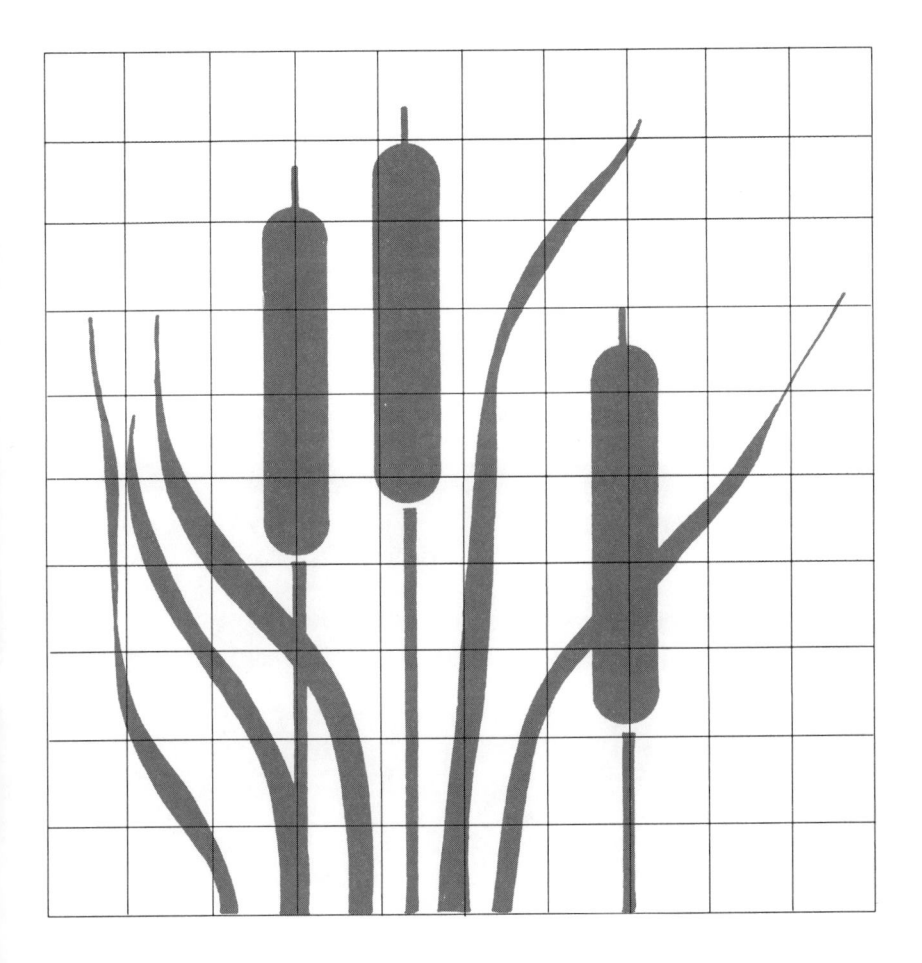

113

The Plant World:
Ivy

Forever green, it is a symbol of faithfulness and eternal life.

The Plant World:
Clover

The three-leaved clover is a symbol of the Trinity; four-leaved, good luck.

The Body:
Head

The chief part of the body, representing the whole person, ruling and controlling all of its other members.

The Body:
Eye

Symbol for the all-knowing, ever-present God.

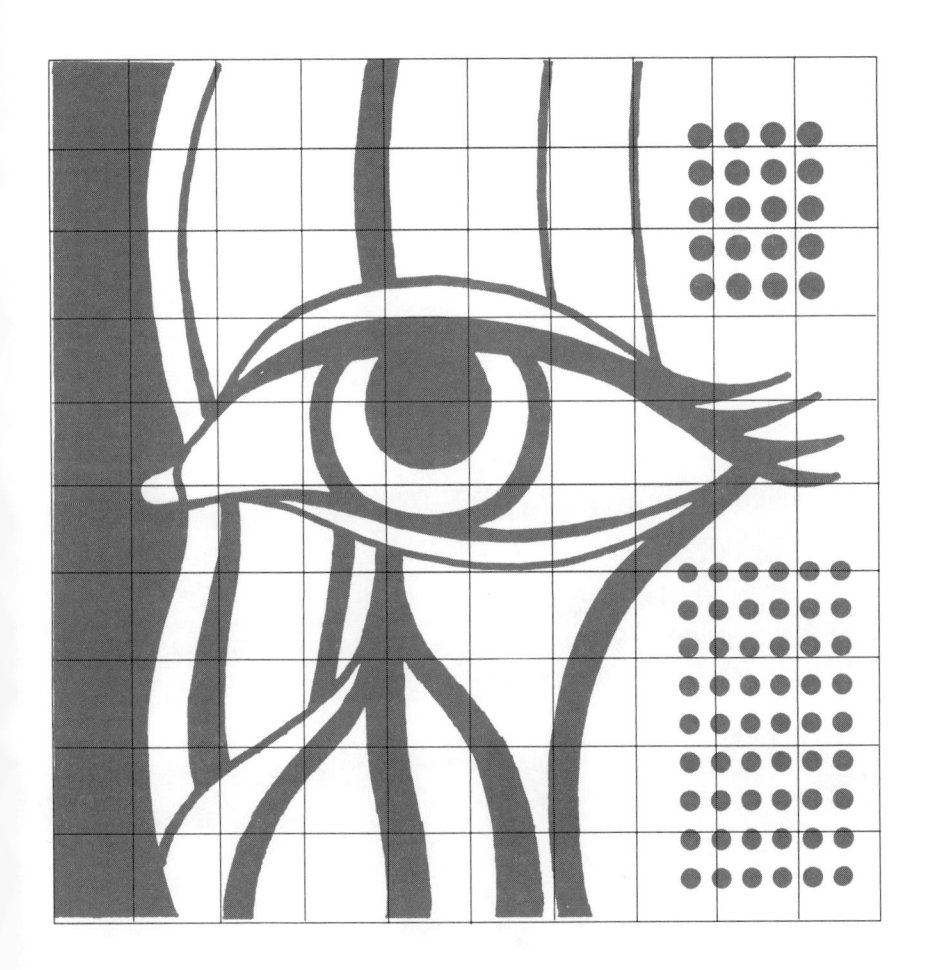

The Body:
Ear

A symbol of Christ's betrayal.

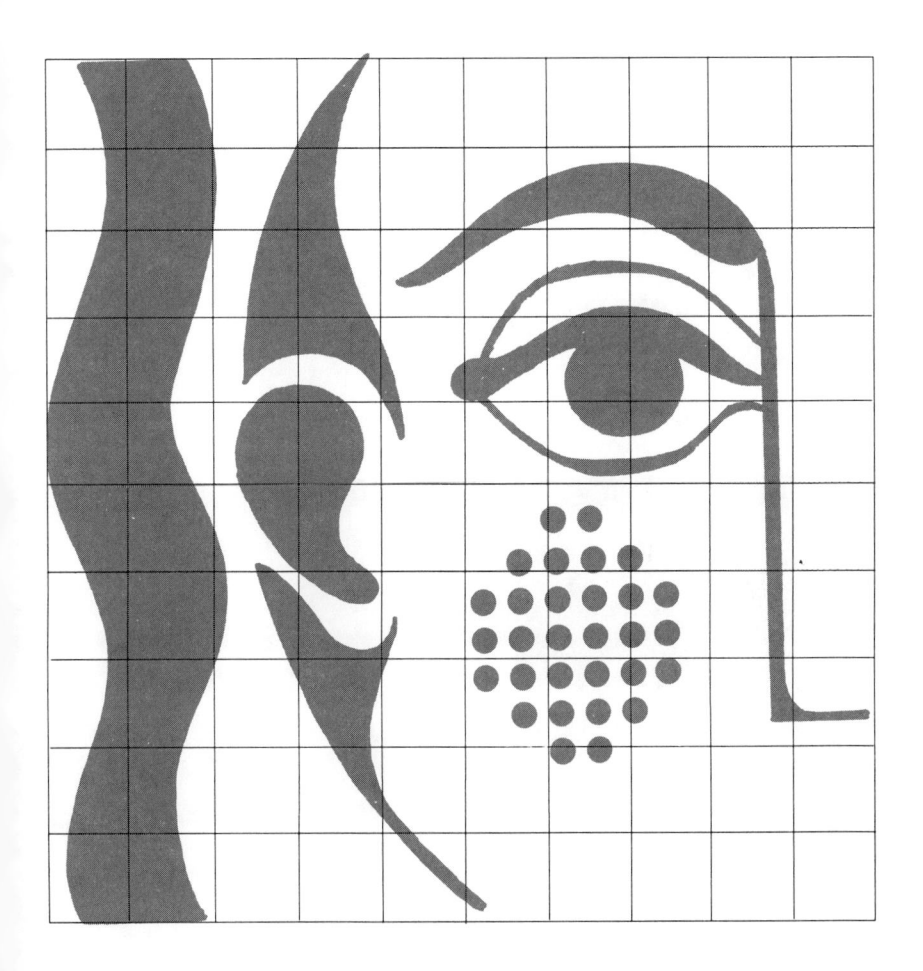

123

The Body:
Hair

A symbol of penitence, with Magdalene as the source.

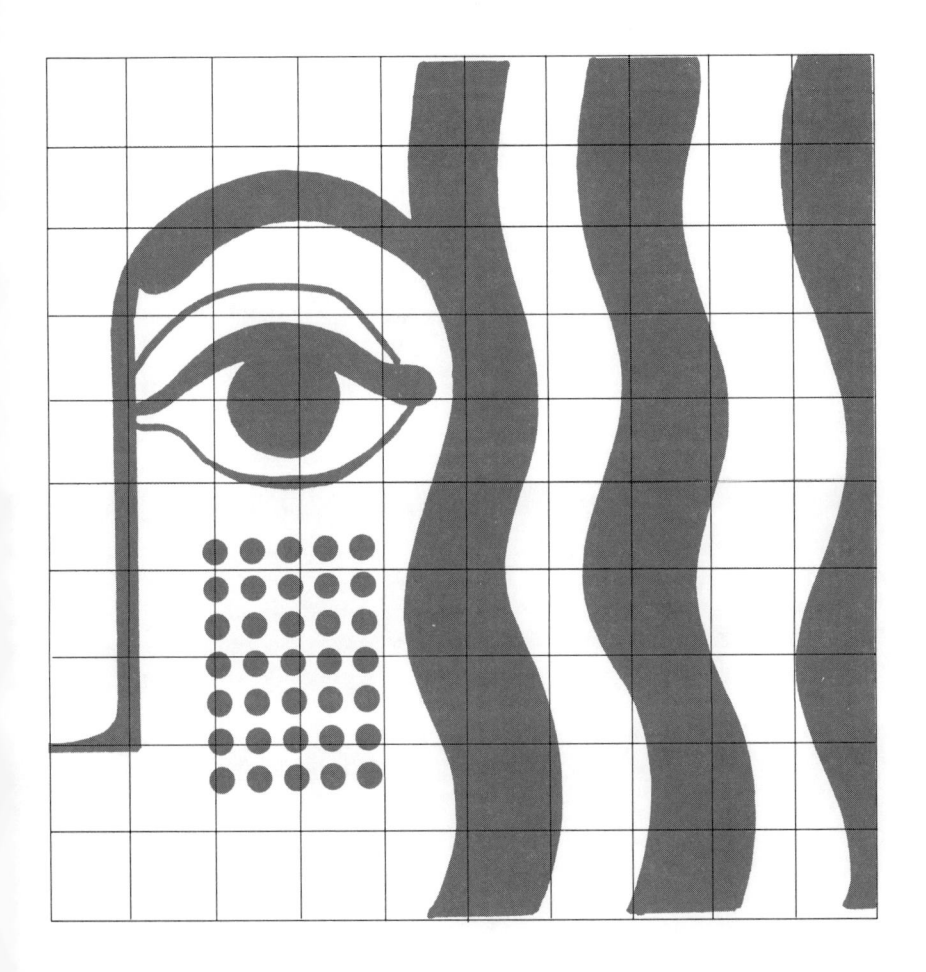

The Body:
Heart

The source of love, joy, and understanding.

The Body:
Hand

Scripture refers to the Lord's hand and arm as symbols of his almighty power and will.

The Body:
Foot

The foot, since it touches the ground, is thought to be the symbol of humility and service.

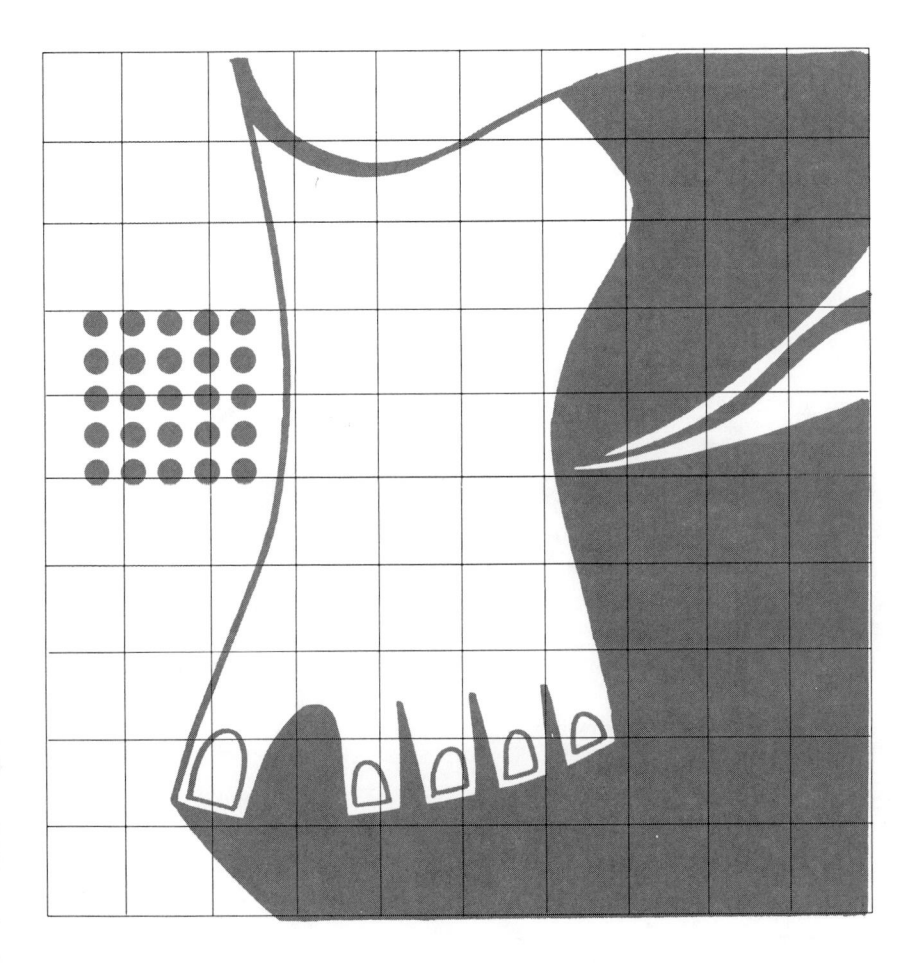

The Body:
Skull

The skull is a symbol of the transitory nature of life here on earth.

The Body:
Stigmata

The five wounds of Christ have been given to certain people of high religious character.

135

PART II
Christian Symbolism from the quilt designs of the Early American period

"Search the Bible" was the motto of the Early American homemakers. And search they did, looking for inspiration for their handmade, pieced quilts, recognized today as genuine examples of a prized American art form.

Unable to fill their churches with forbidden decorative images, they satisfied their creative instincts with needle and thread and found solace in extracting from the Bible inspiration for quilts, water colors, marriage and birth certificates. The titles given to the quilt squares shown here are authentic. Even though they may seem awkward, sometimes stilted, or totally irrelevant to the subject matter, we can only assume that from the quilt- makers' Bible readings or from an inherited legend, this was an educated or inspired choice of words to describe their handiwork.

The beauty of these designs is that even though they have a religious base and imaginative titles, they consist of wonderful linear and abstract patterns that can be used in their original form, or they can be abstracted in composition and color to be used in today's liturgy.

The original quilts were, of course, sewn together with various pieces of patterned and colored calico. You can certainly pursue this route in constructing your banners, but I would strongly encourage you to interpret the designs in contemporary color schemes. Amish quilts have a beautiful sense of color combinations, and I suggest you study their designs as well as the graphic designers' approach to color listed in the bibliography.

The Universe:
Search the Bible

Learning comes through the word and the image, through the mind and the heart. The Early American quilter searched the Bible for inspiration.

The Universe:
Sunshine

Sunshine dispels the clouds and darkness of sin and error.

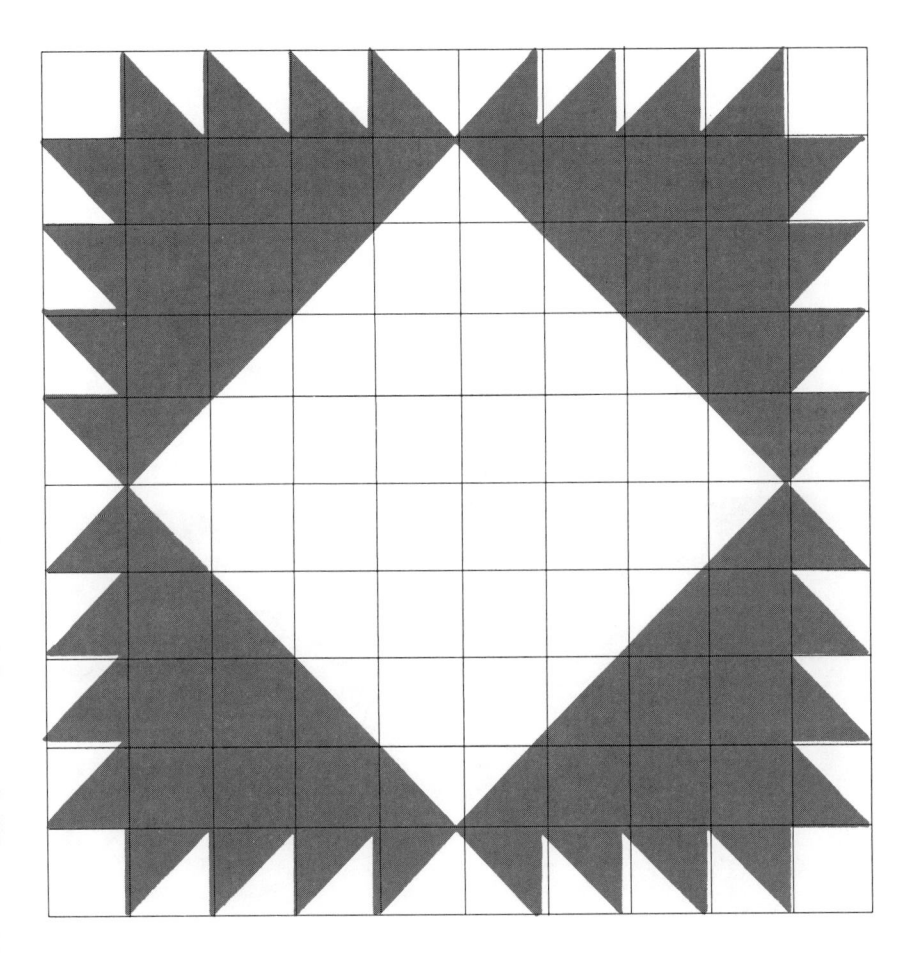

The Universe:
Sunlight and Darkness

Darkness casts doubts, but sunlight lights up the truth.

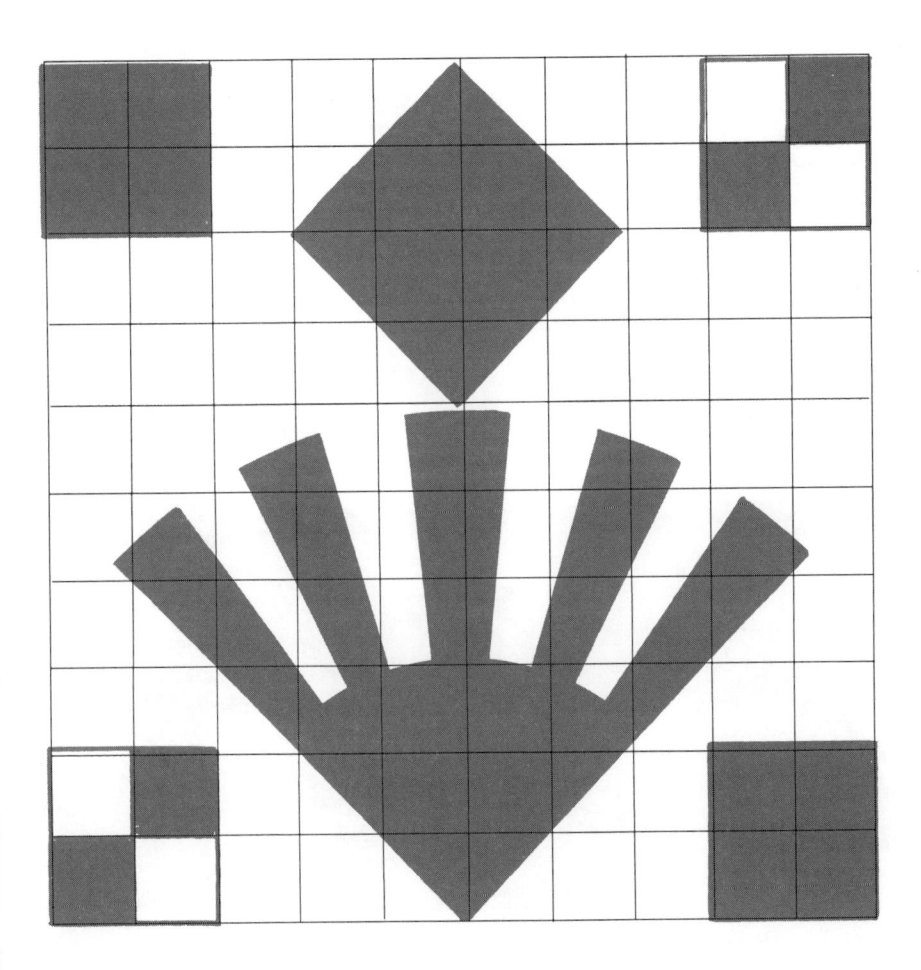

143

The Universe:
Sunshine and Shadow

Some believe that all of our lives depend upon the motion of celestial bodies to help us in God's command.

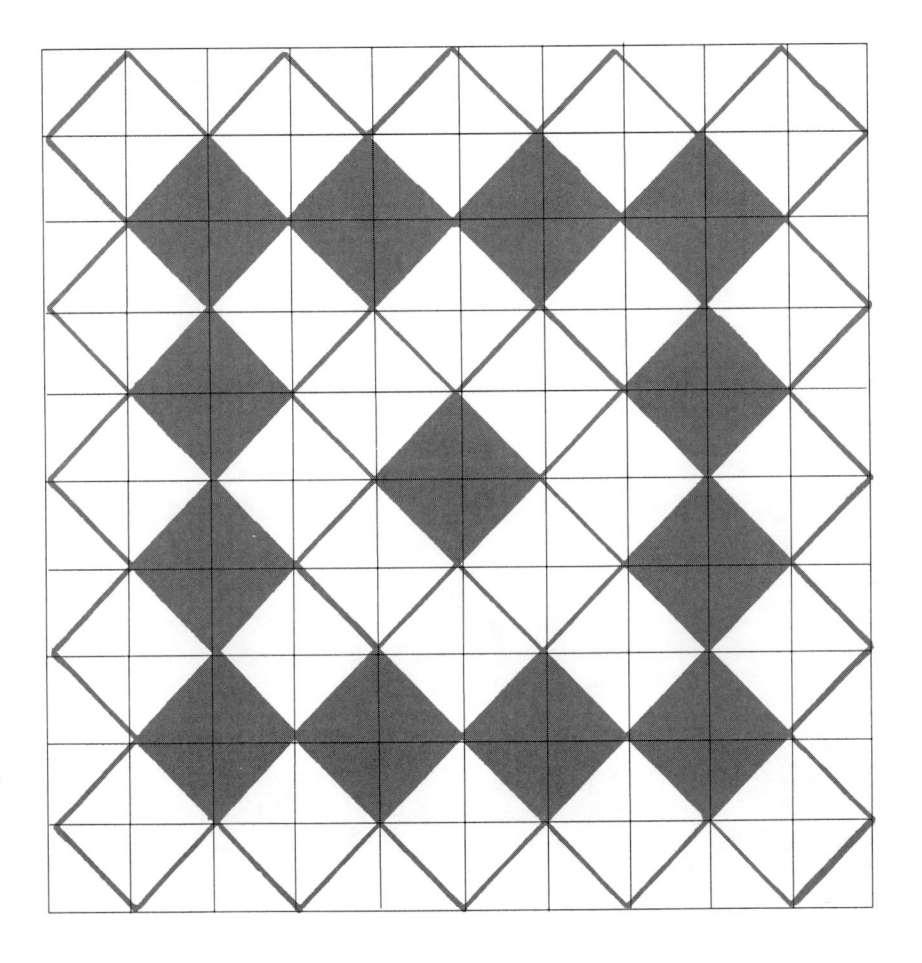

Sunshine and Shadow

The Universe:
Star

The sun, moon, and stars are all part of the city of Heaven.

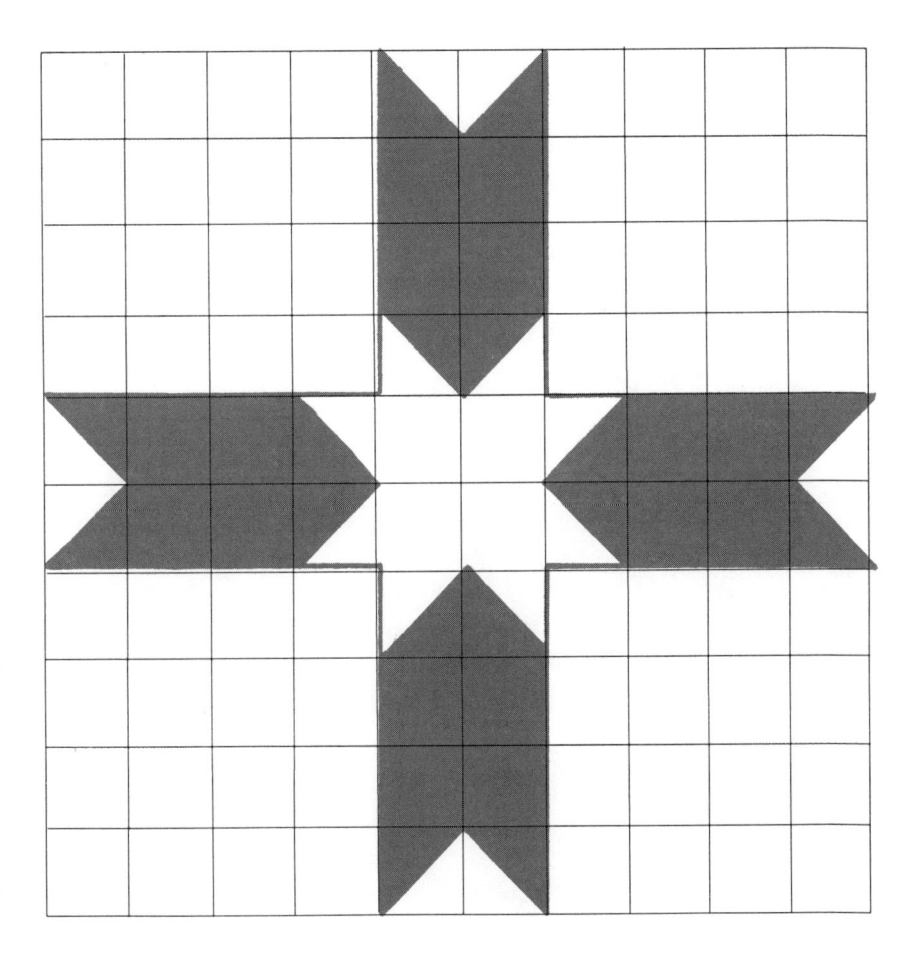

The Old Testament:
Garden of Eden

And the Lord planted a garden eastward in Eden (Genesis 2:8).

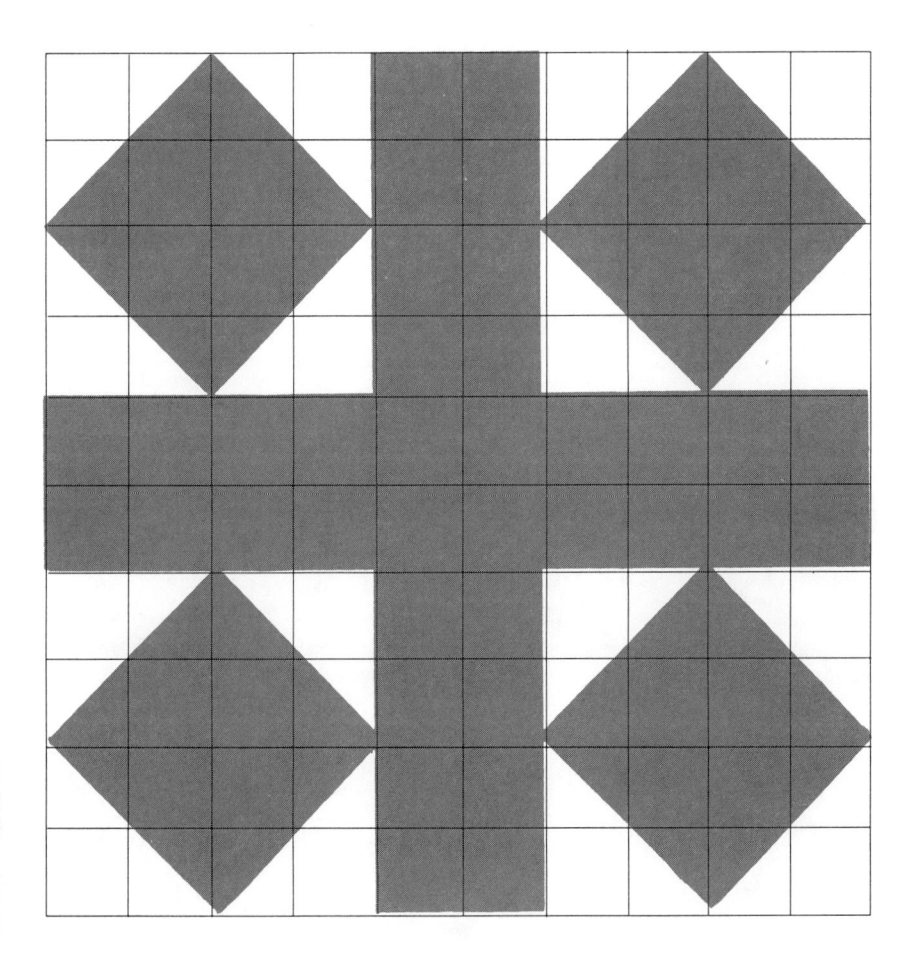

The Old Testament:
Tree of Life

The tree of life, like the human heart, grows best in an orderly garden separated from the cares of the world.

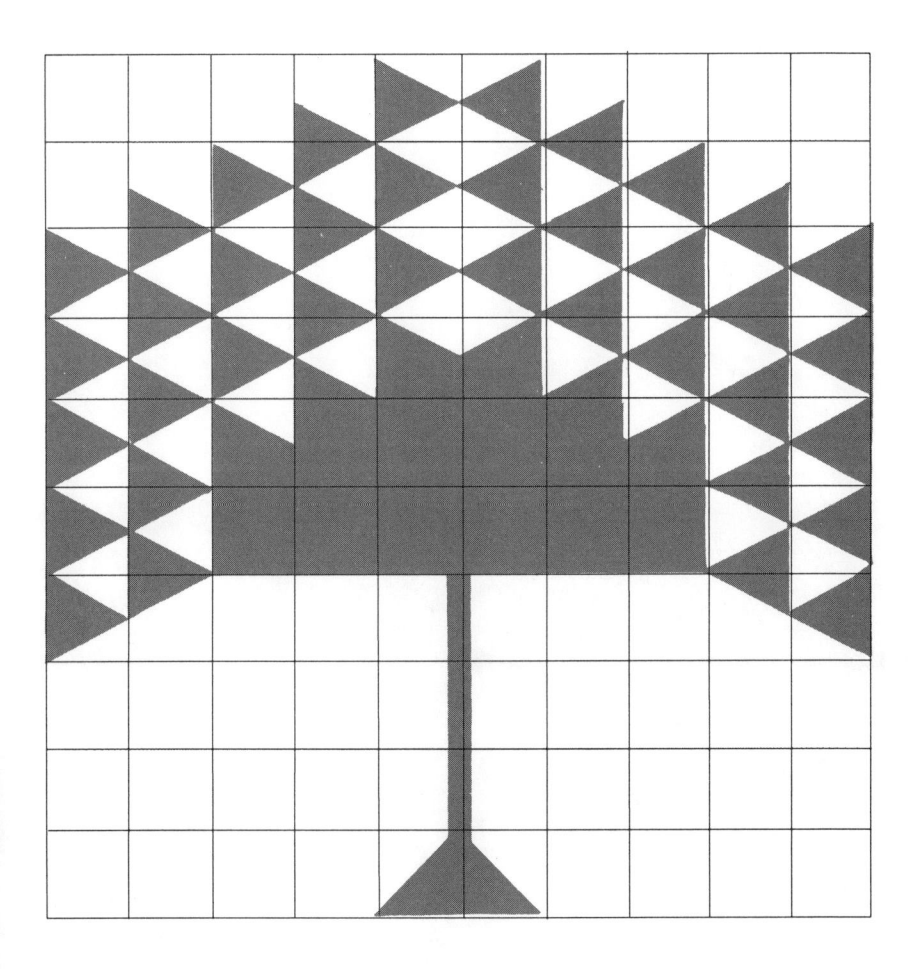

The Old Testament:
Children of Israel

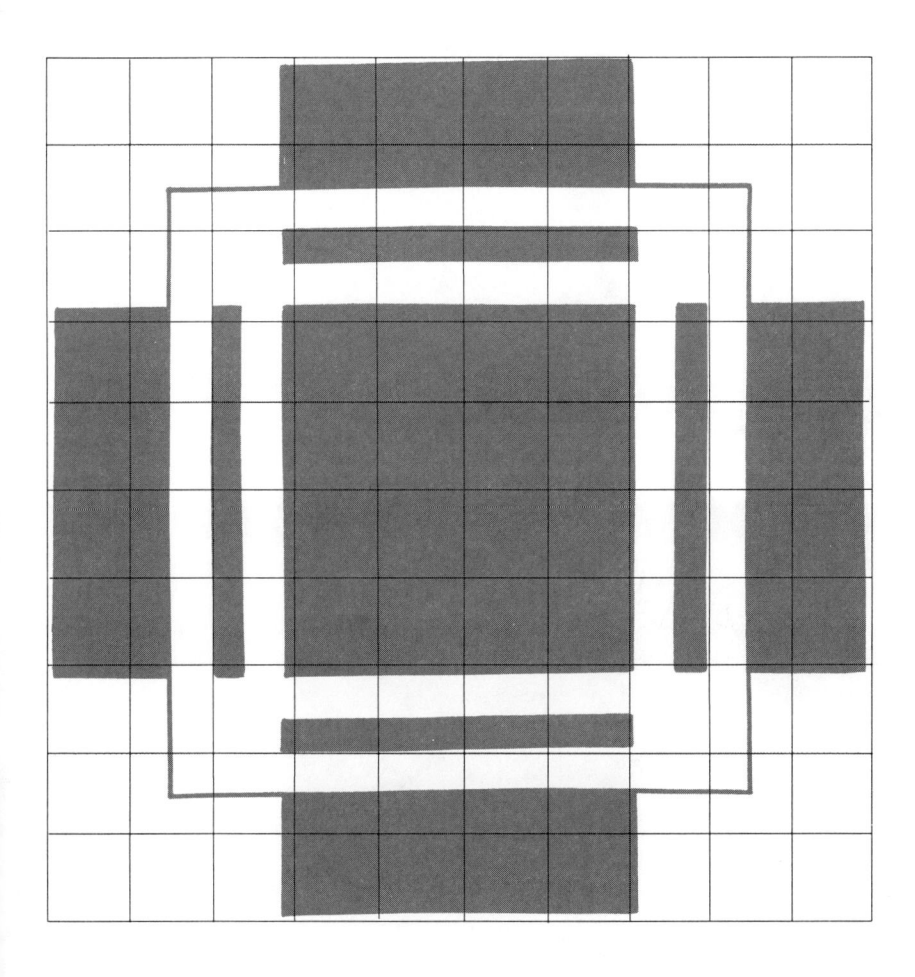

153

The Old Testament:
Jacob's Ladder

...and behold a ladder set up on the earth, and the top of it reached to Heaven (Genesis 28:12).

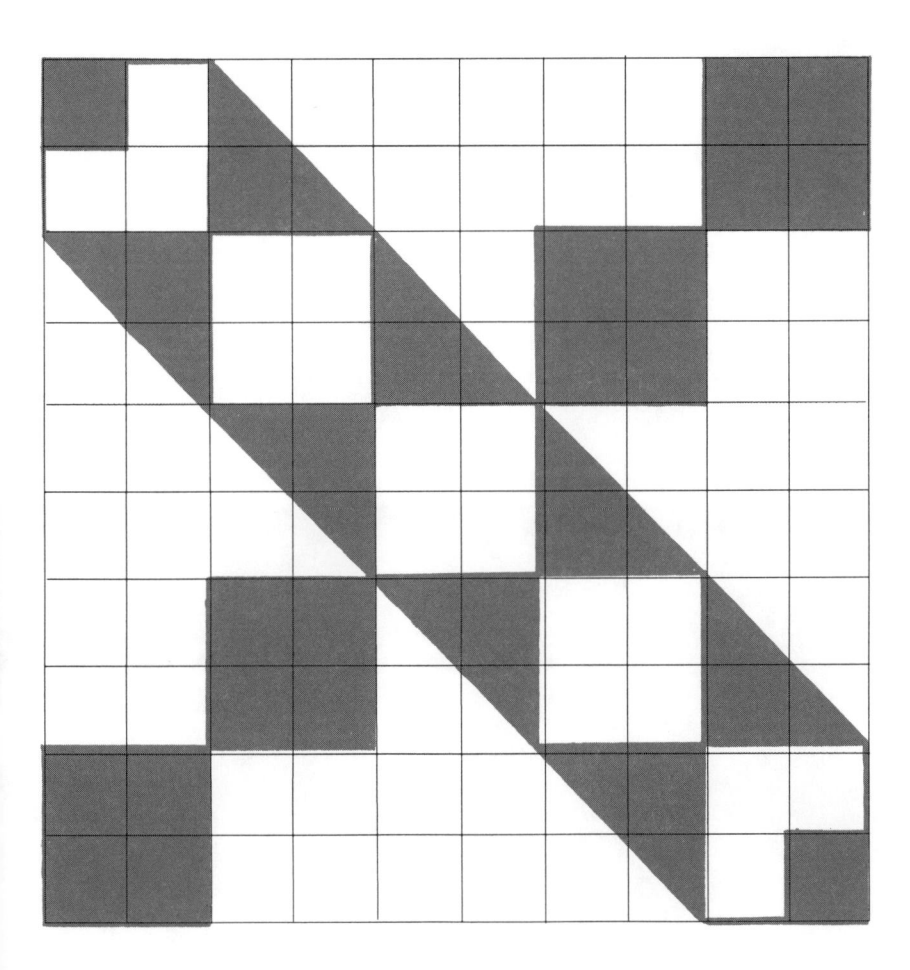

The Old Testament:
David and Goliath

So David prevailed over the Philistine (1 Samuel 17:50).

The Old Testament:
Job's Tears

Satan smote Job with sore boils from the sole of his foot unto his crown (Job 2:7).

The Old Testament:
Job's Troubles

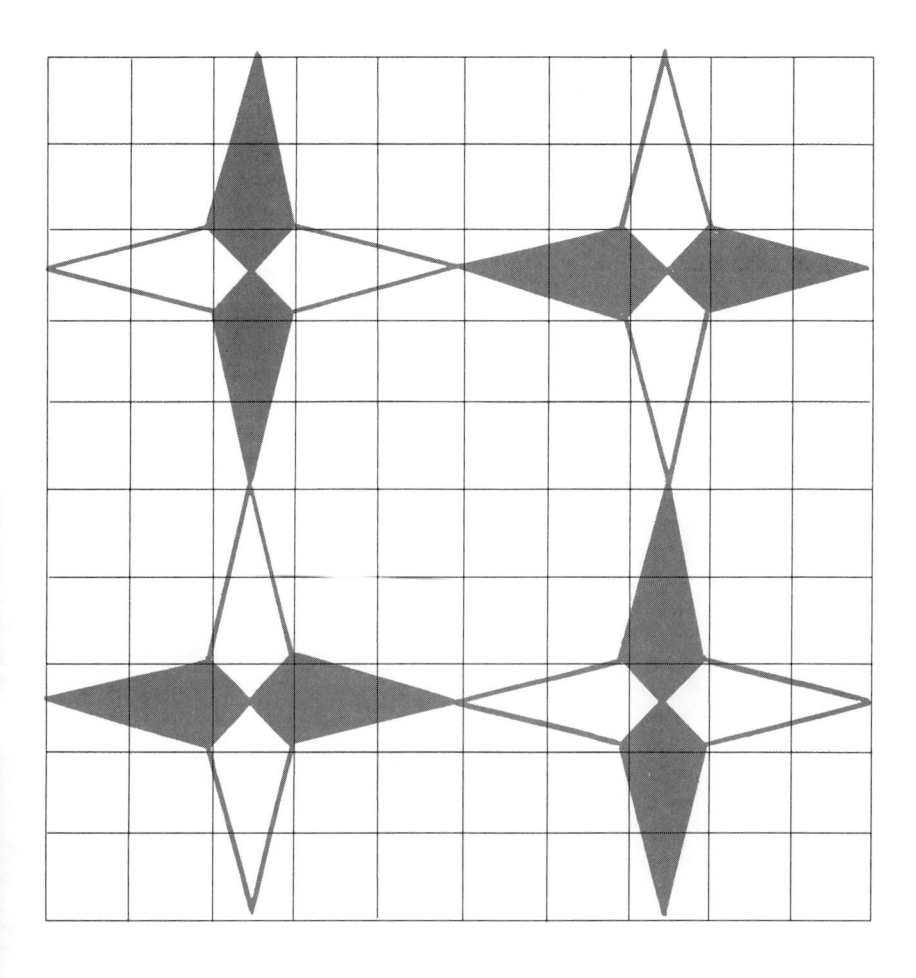

The Old Testament:
Joseph's Coat

...and he made him a coat of many colors (Genesis 37:3).

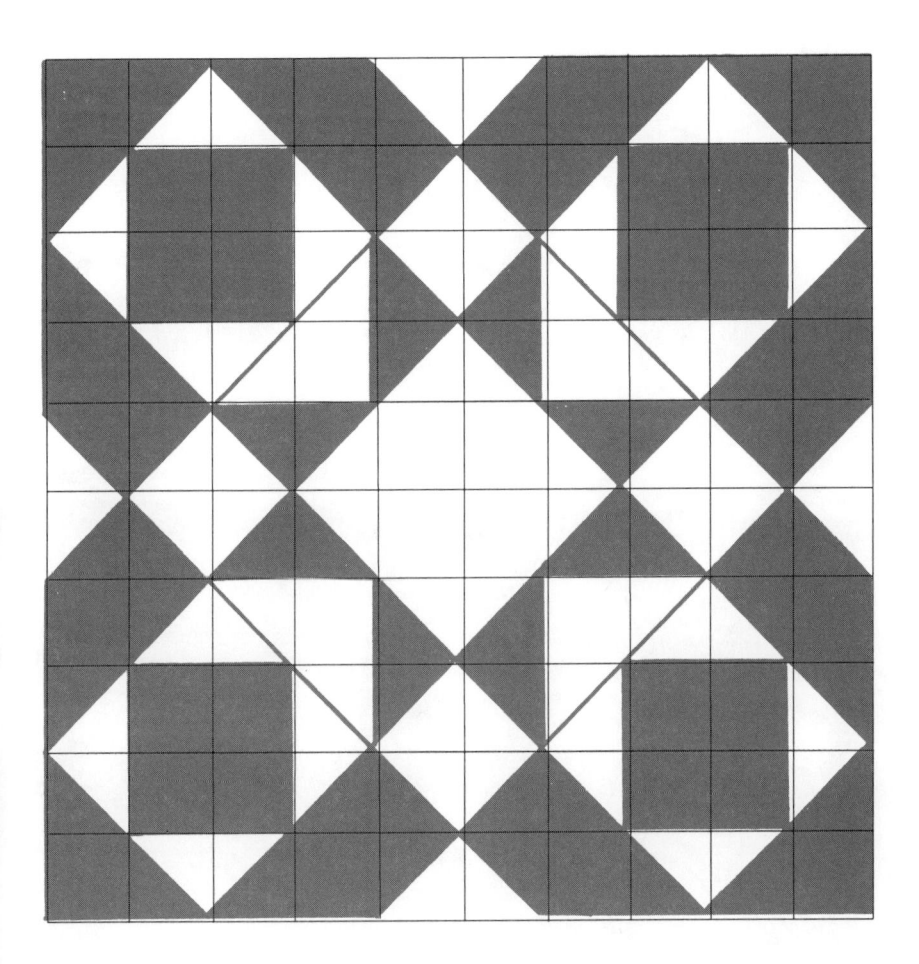

The Old Testament:
Bear's Claws

The bear, a wild animal, was a symbol of cruelty and possibly evil influence.

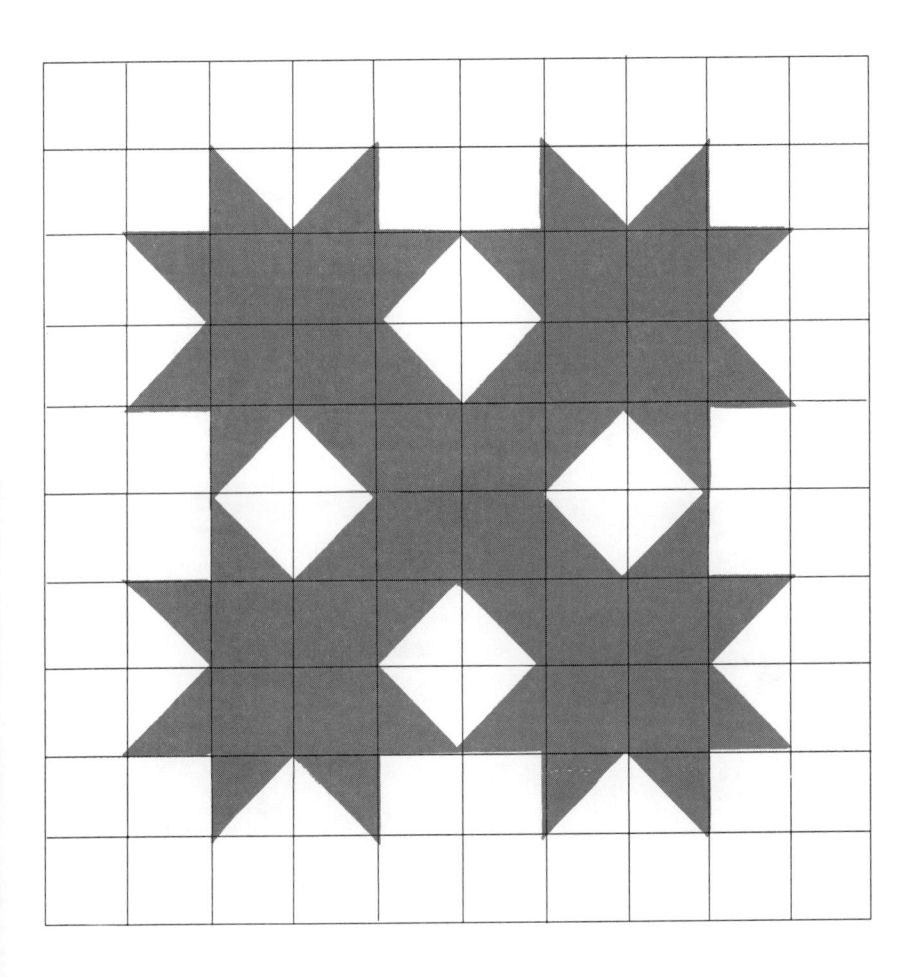

The Old Testament:
Which Way?

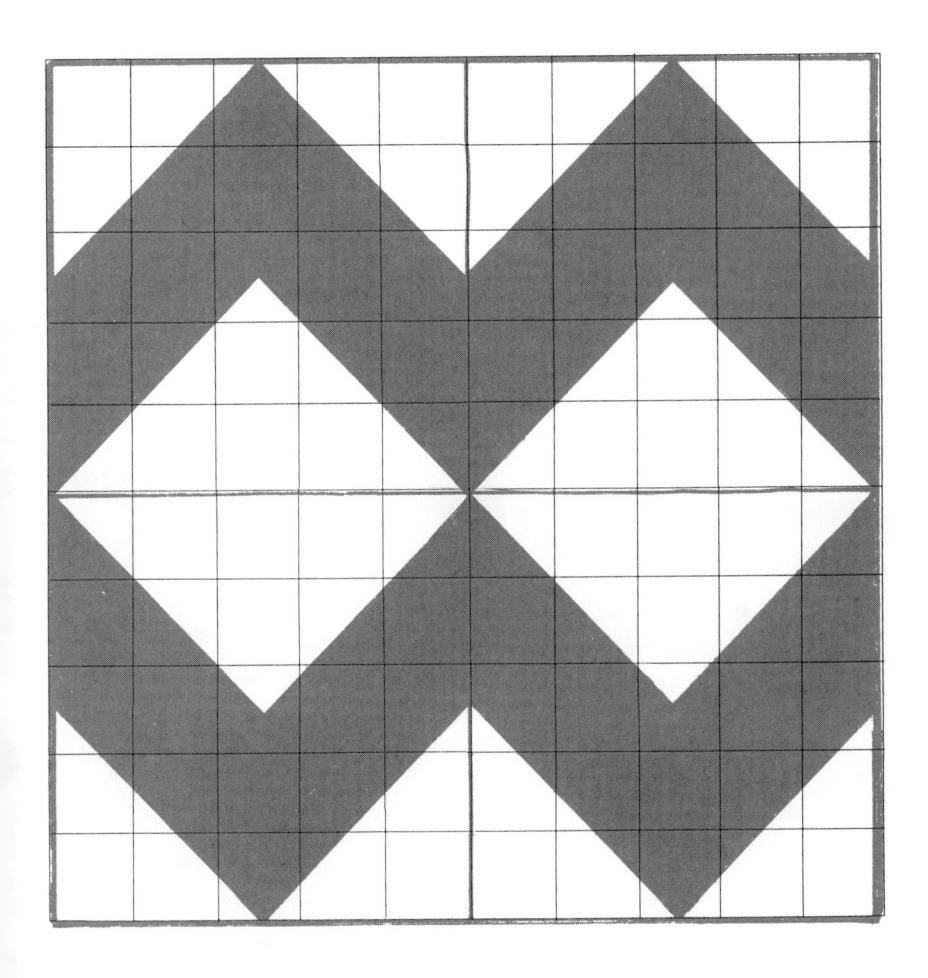

The Animal World:
Birds
The time of singing birds has come (Song of Solomon 2:11-12).

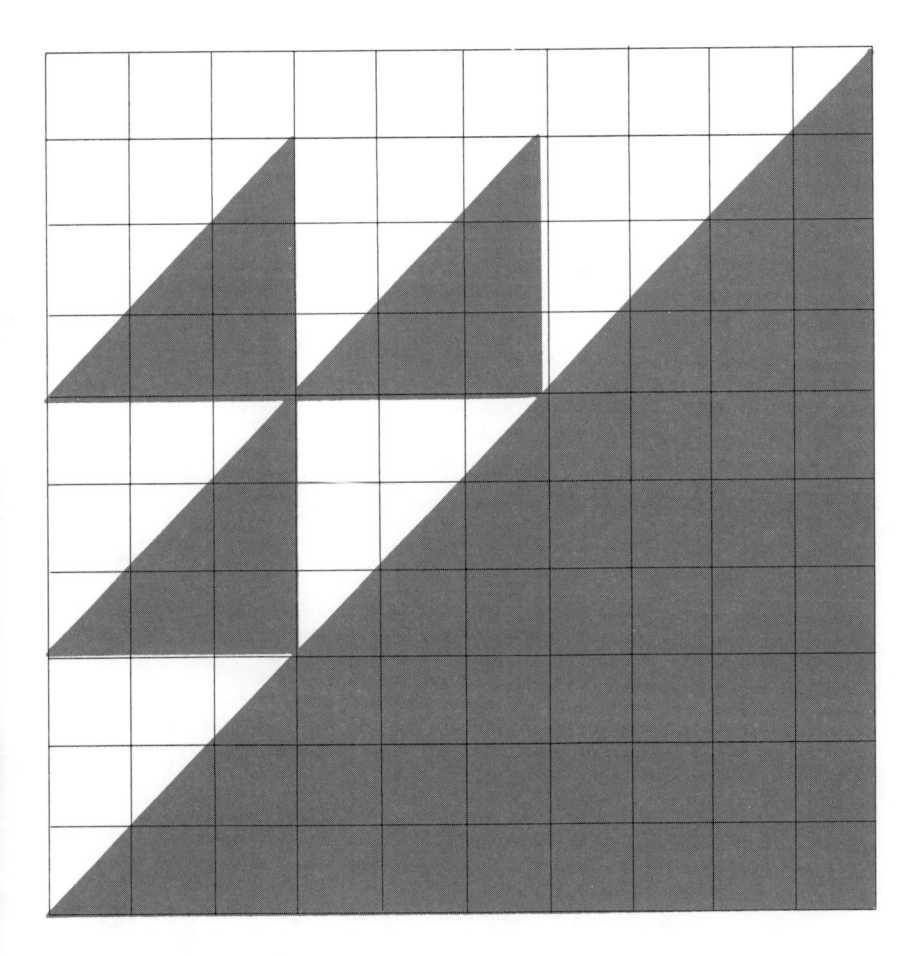

The Animal World:
Honey Bee

A symbol of the Christian and his/her activity.

The Animal World:
Butterfly

A symbol of the Resurrection.

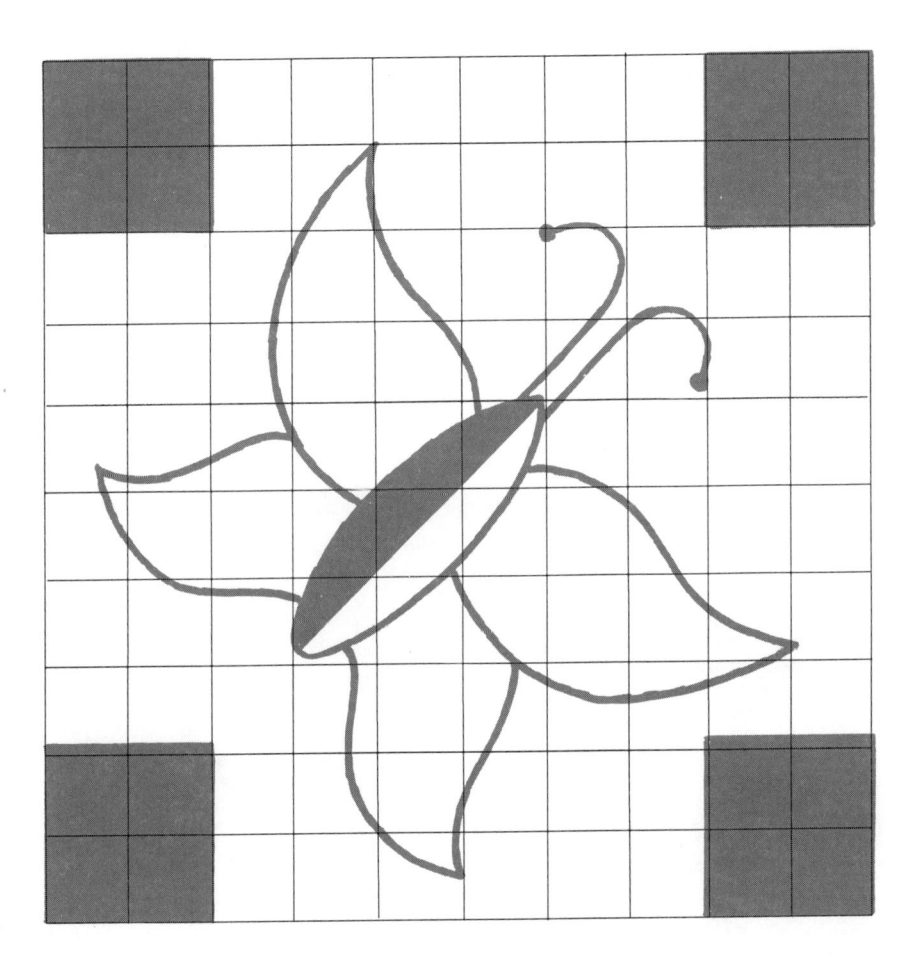

The Animal World:
Snail's Trail

A symbol of the sinner.

The Animal World:
Dove

A symbol of purity and peace.

The Plant World:
Lily

The lily represents the divine body, which provides the nectar of life.

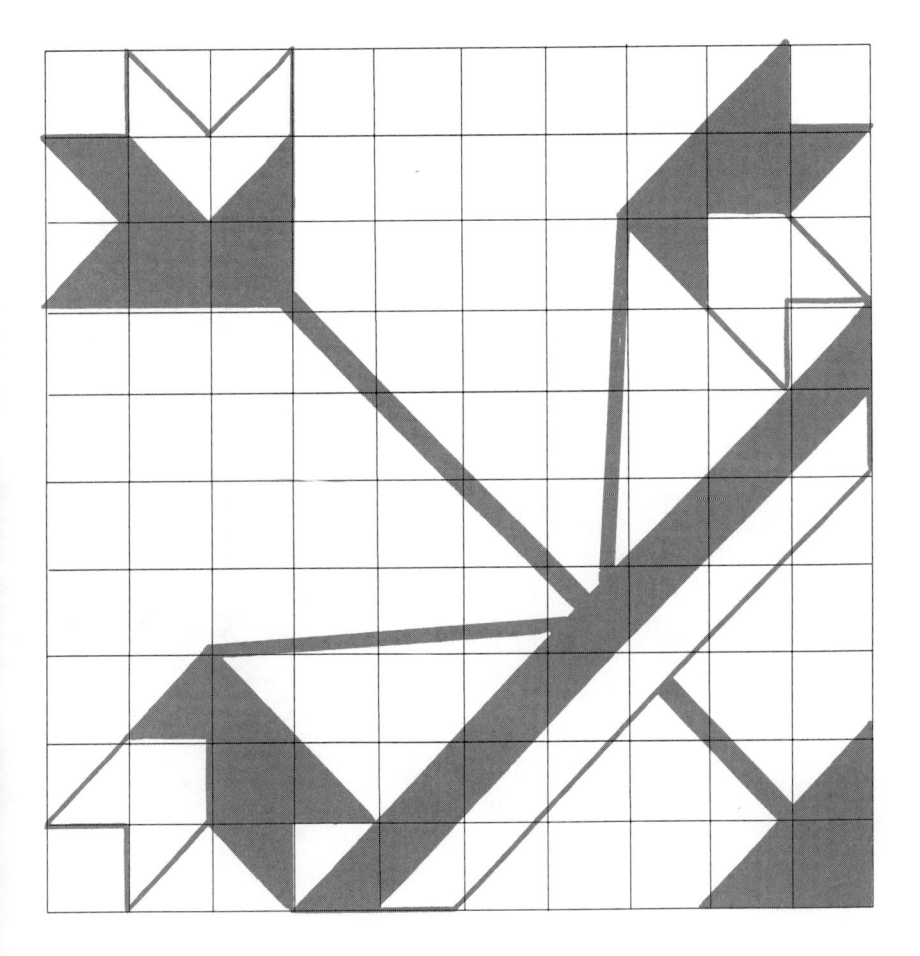

The Plant World:
Rose

A symbol of the good life when Jesus returns.

The Plant World:
Grapes

Another allusion to the Last Supper and the Passion.

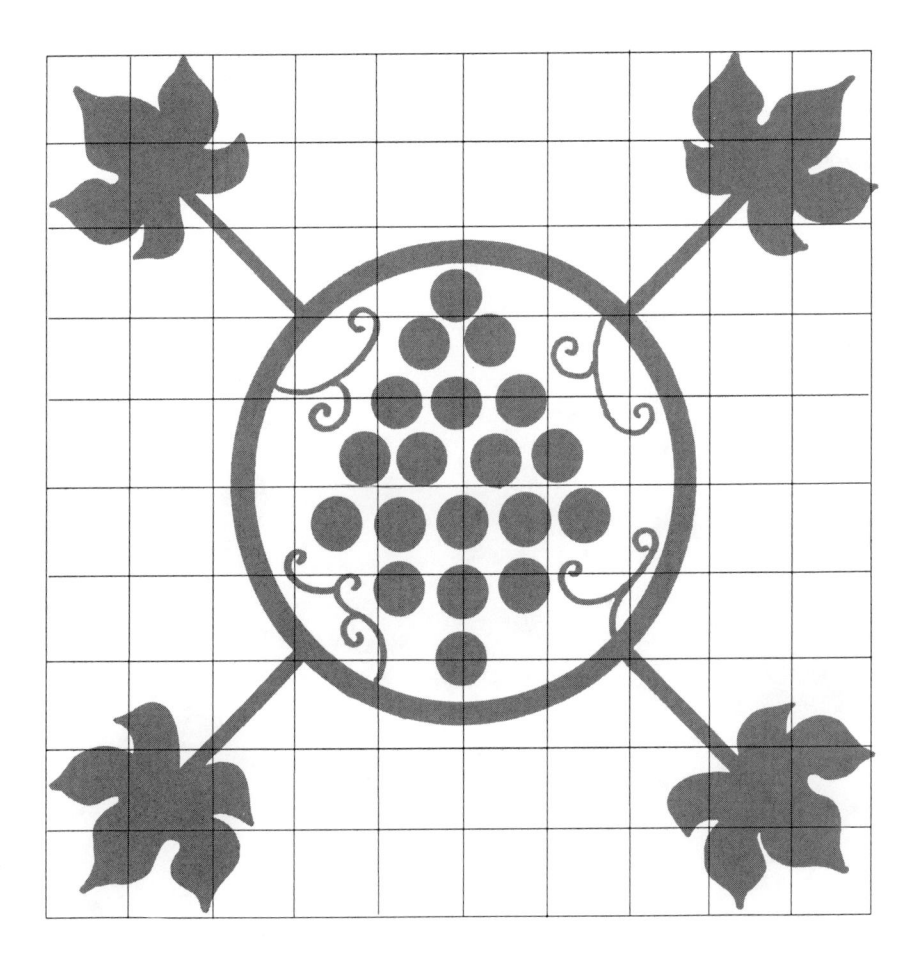

The Plant World:
Hearts and Flowers

Flowers are symbols of virtues, teaching us that everything grows for the honor of God.

The Body:
Next-Door Neighbor

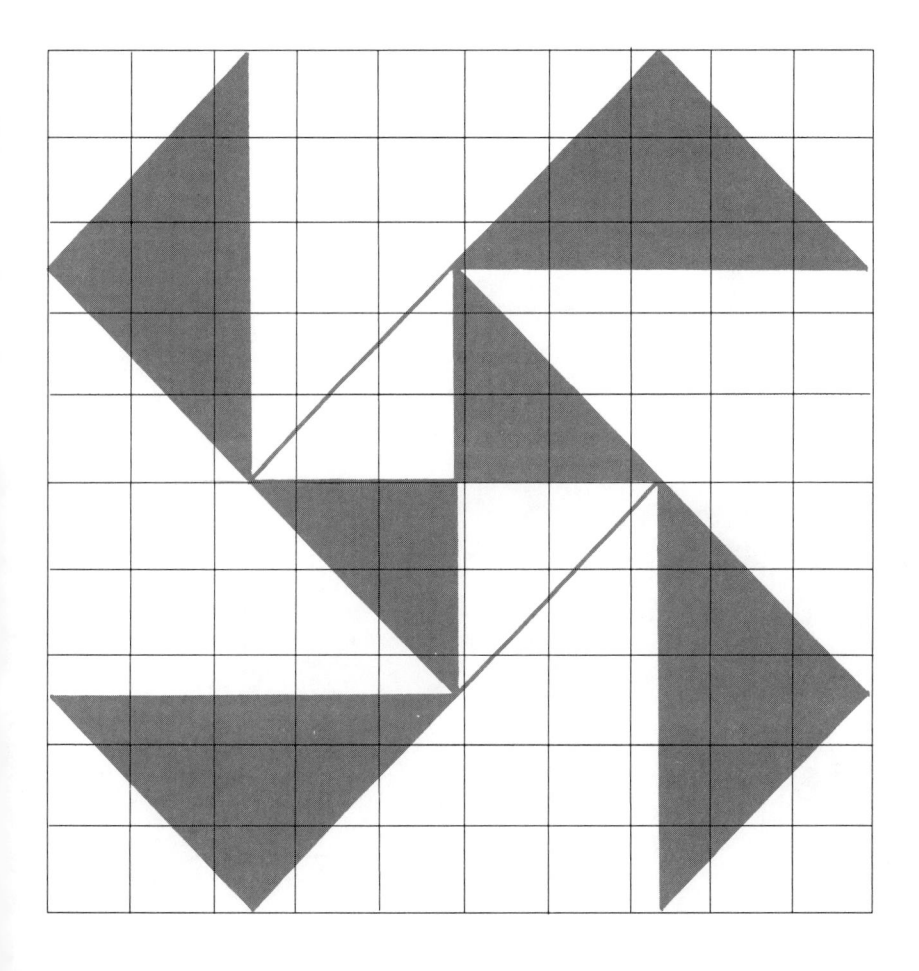

The Body:
Hands to Work, Hearts to God

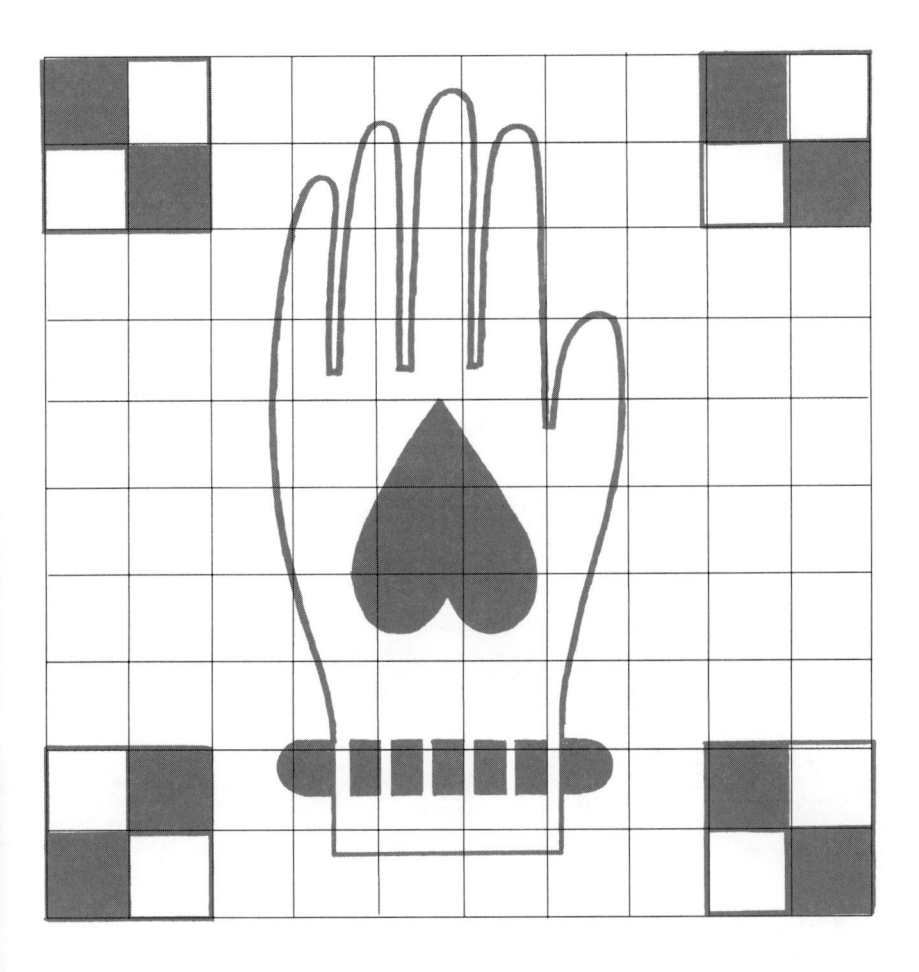

The Body:
Peace and Plenty

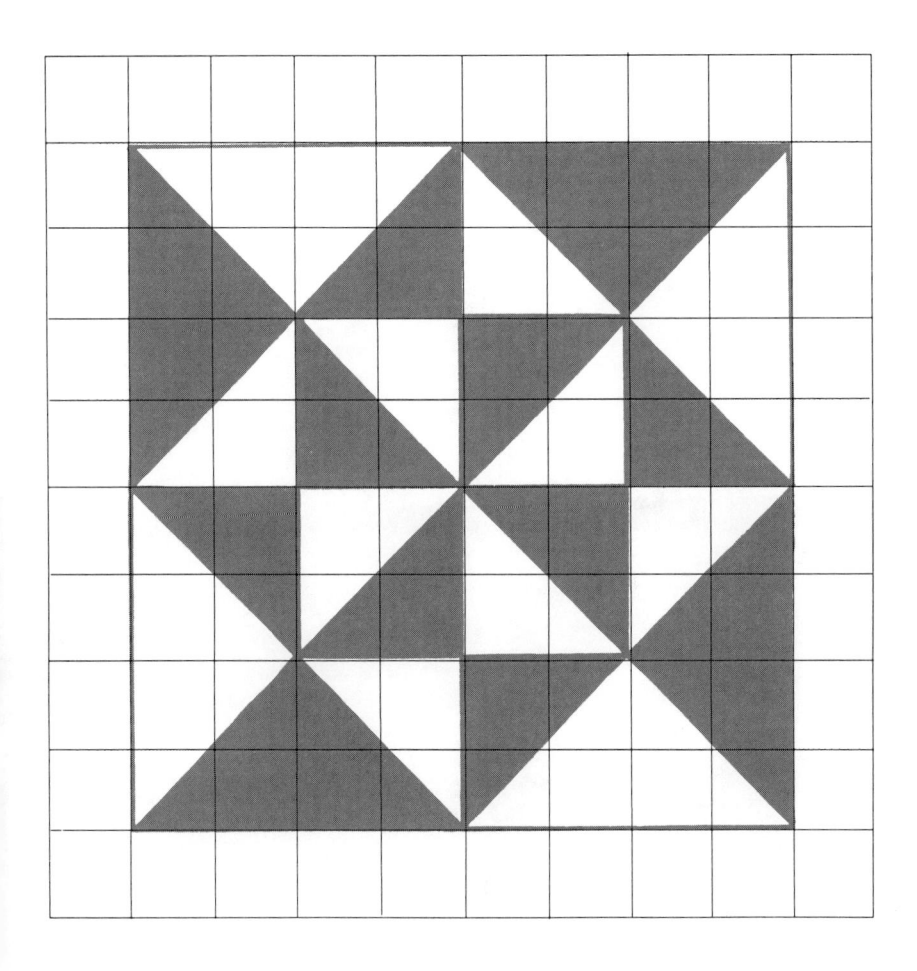

The New Testament:
Star of Bethlehem

And lo, the star, which they saw in the east, went before them (Matthew 2:9).

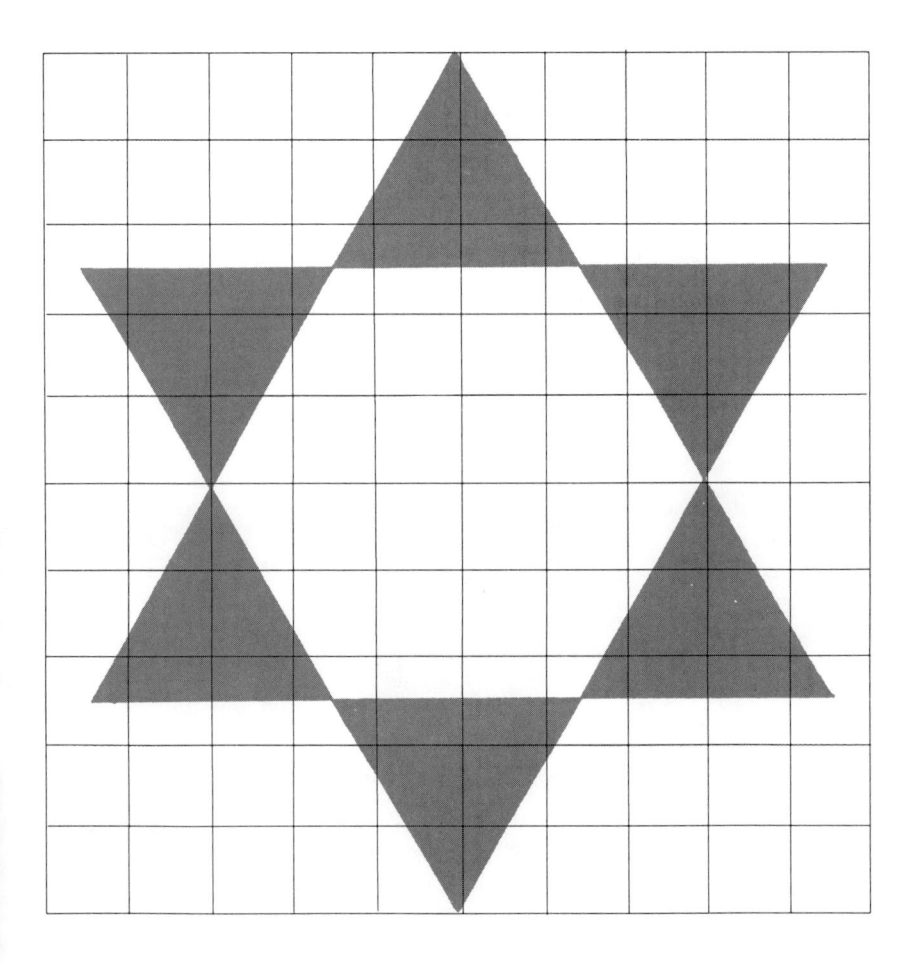

The New Testament:
Christmas Star
The star stood over where the young child was (Matthew 2:9).

The New Testament:
Carpenter's Square

A symbol of St. Joseph, the carpenter.

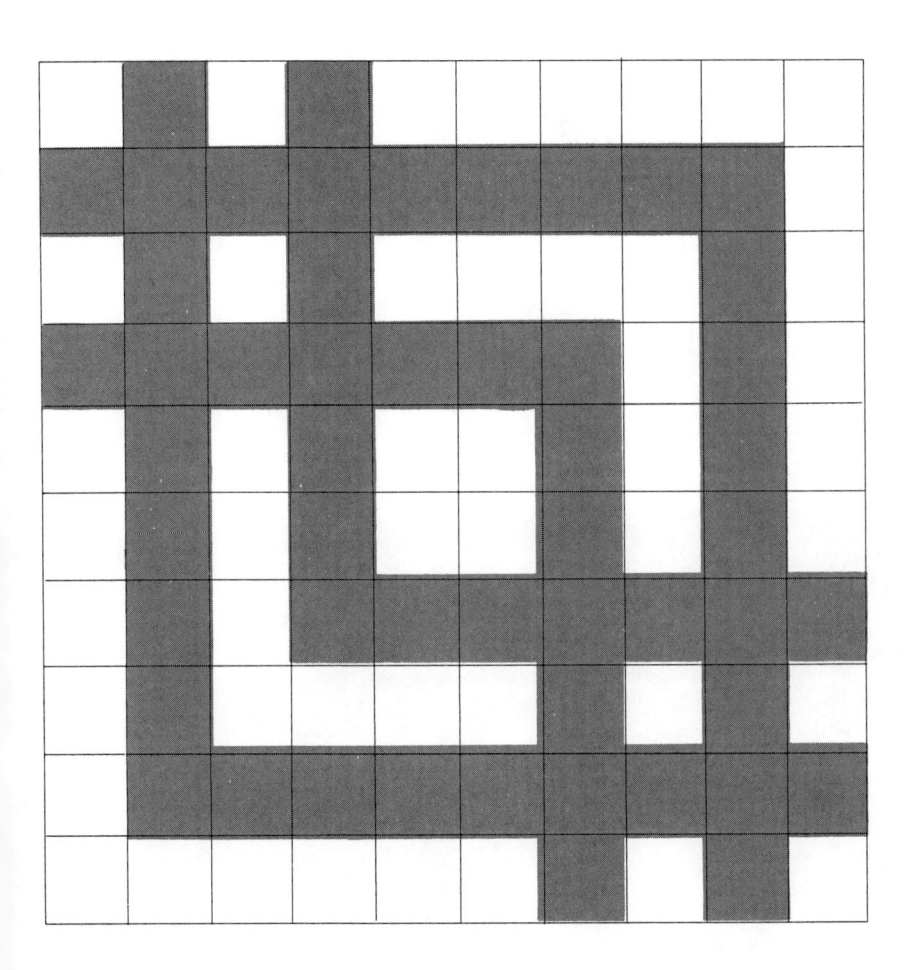

The New Testament:
Diamond and Square

Two carpenter's tools, the diamond and the square are joined together to form one unit, just as God and people.

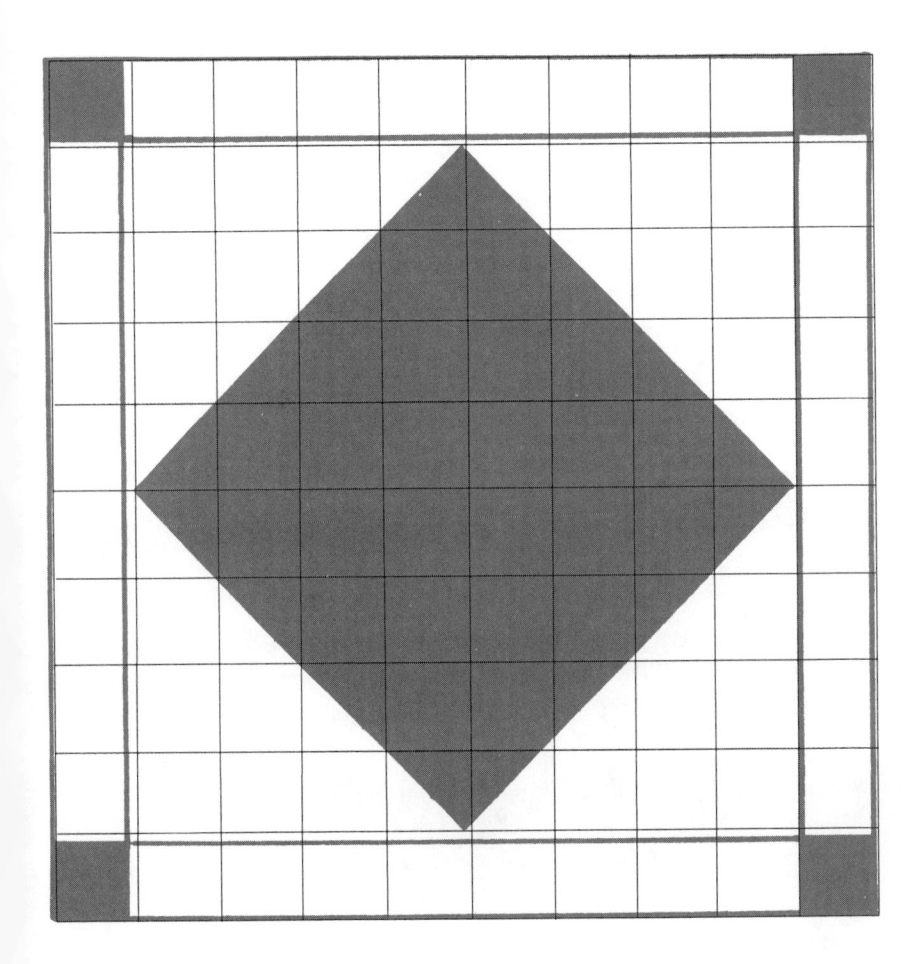

The New Testament:
Tree of Temptation

And the devil, taking him up into a high mountain (Luke 4:5-8).

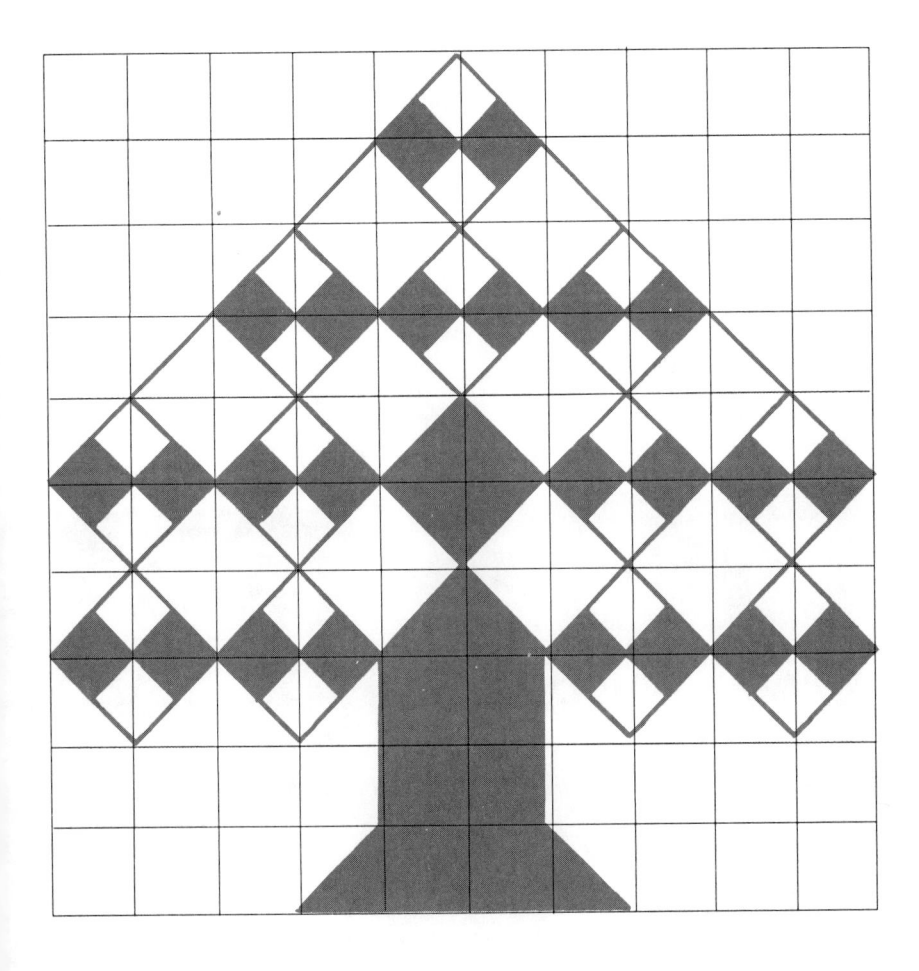

The New Testament:
Grape Basket

Symbol of the wine at the Last Supper.

The New Testament:
Hosanna

They took branches of palm leaves and went forth to meet him (John 12:13).

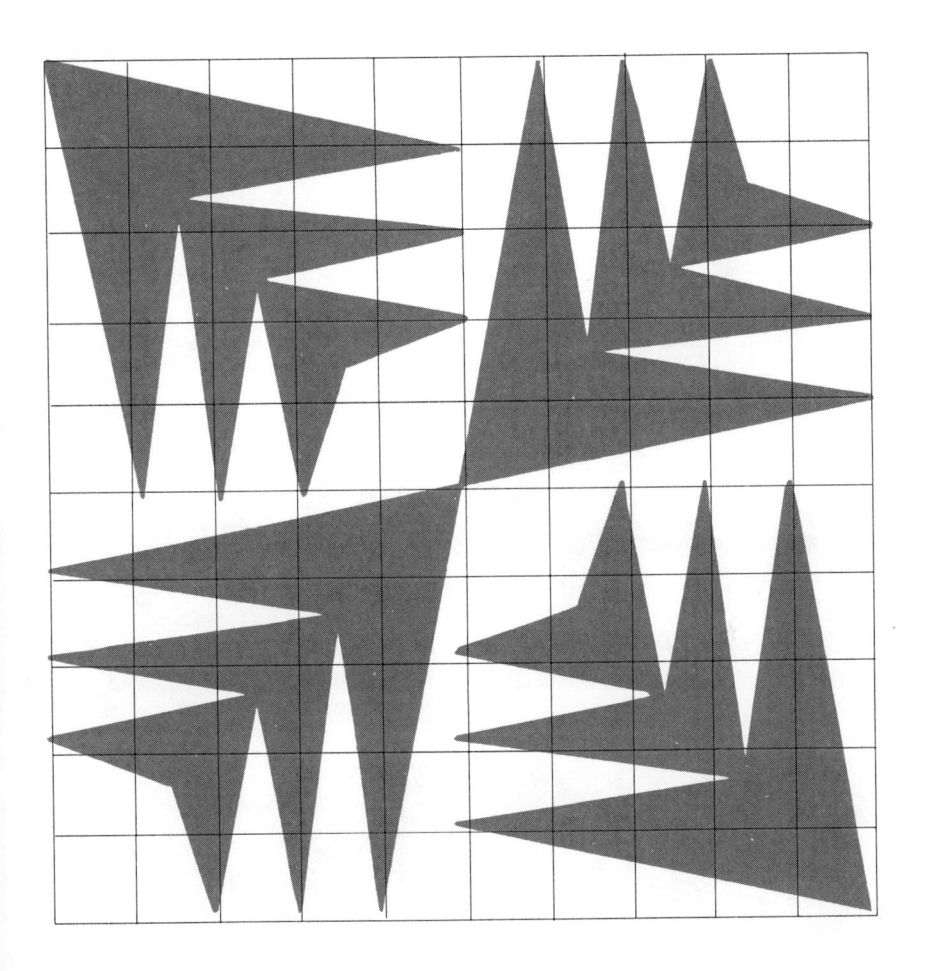

The New Testament:
King's Crown

Blessed is the King of Israel that cometh in the name of the Lord (John 12:13).

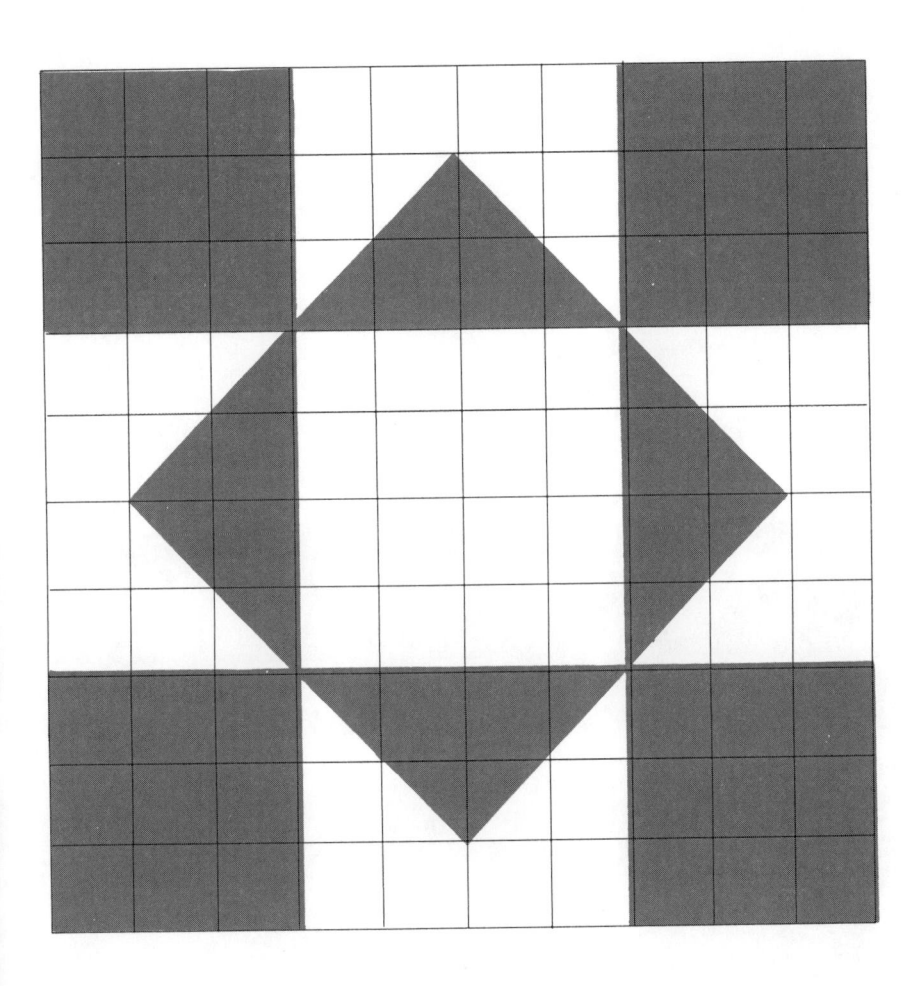

The New Testament:
Caesar's Crown

Render therefore unto Caesar... (Matthew 12:21).

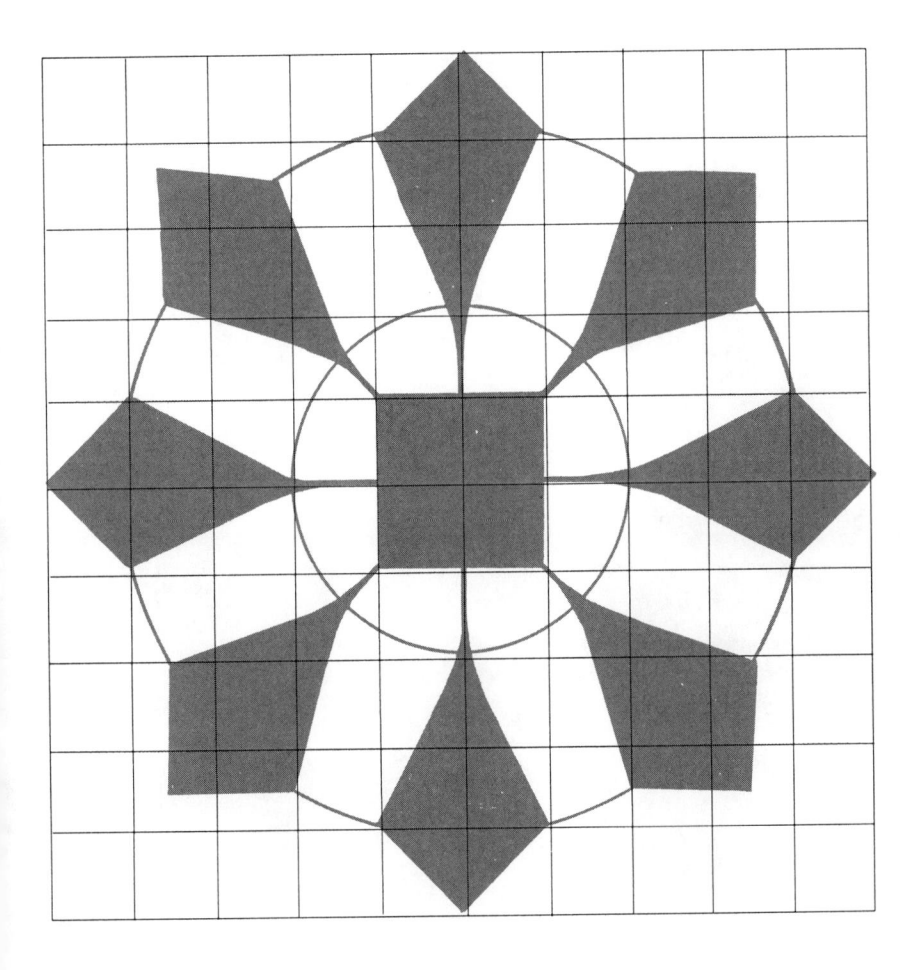

The New Testament:
Crown of Thorns

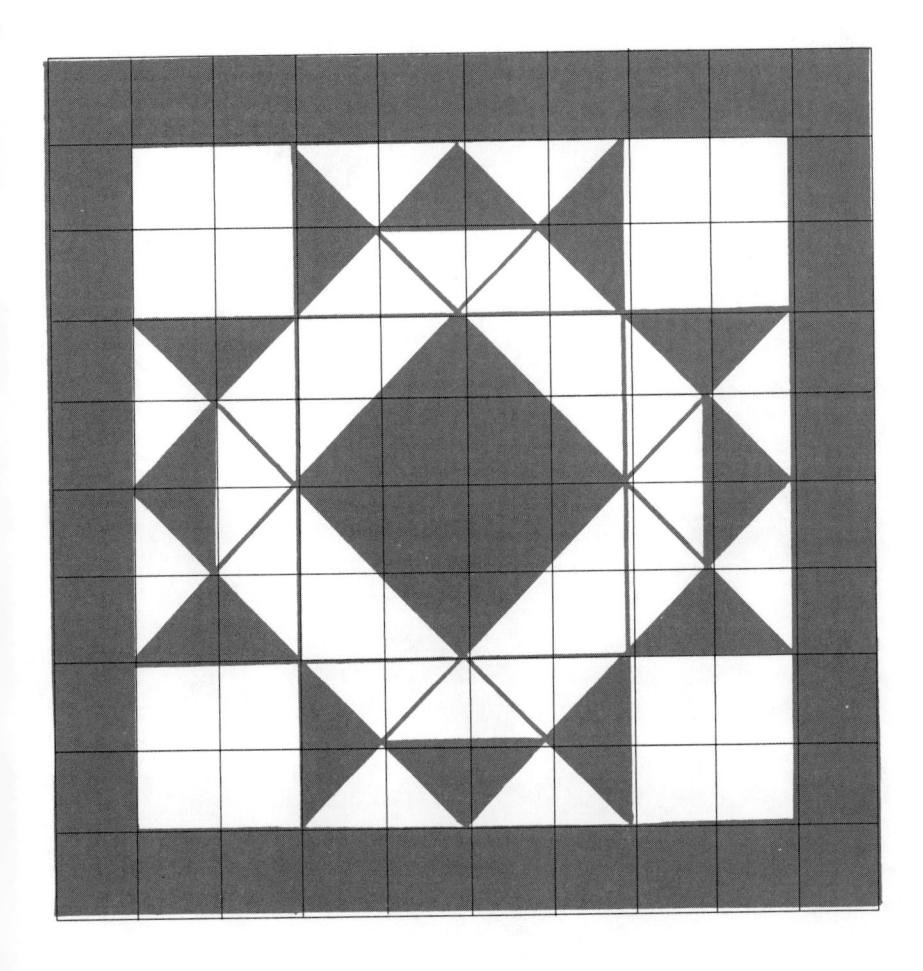

The New Testament:
Crown and Cross

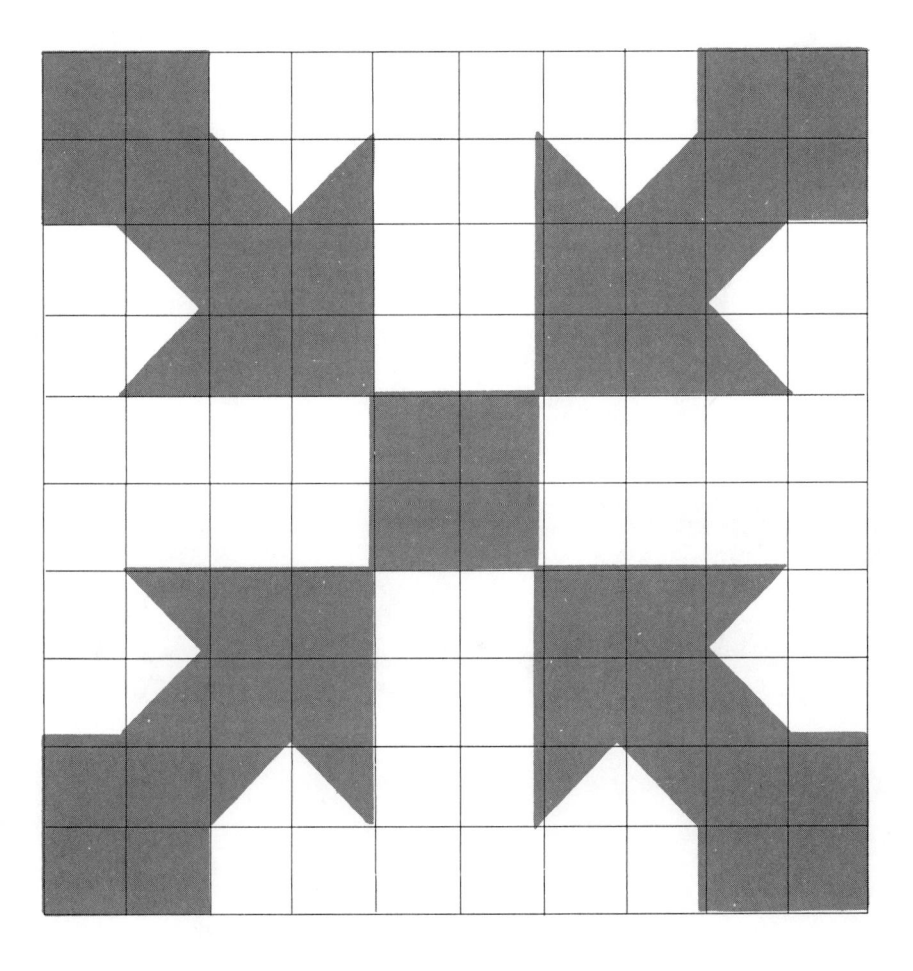

The New Testament:
Cross and Crown

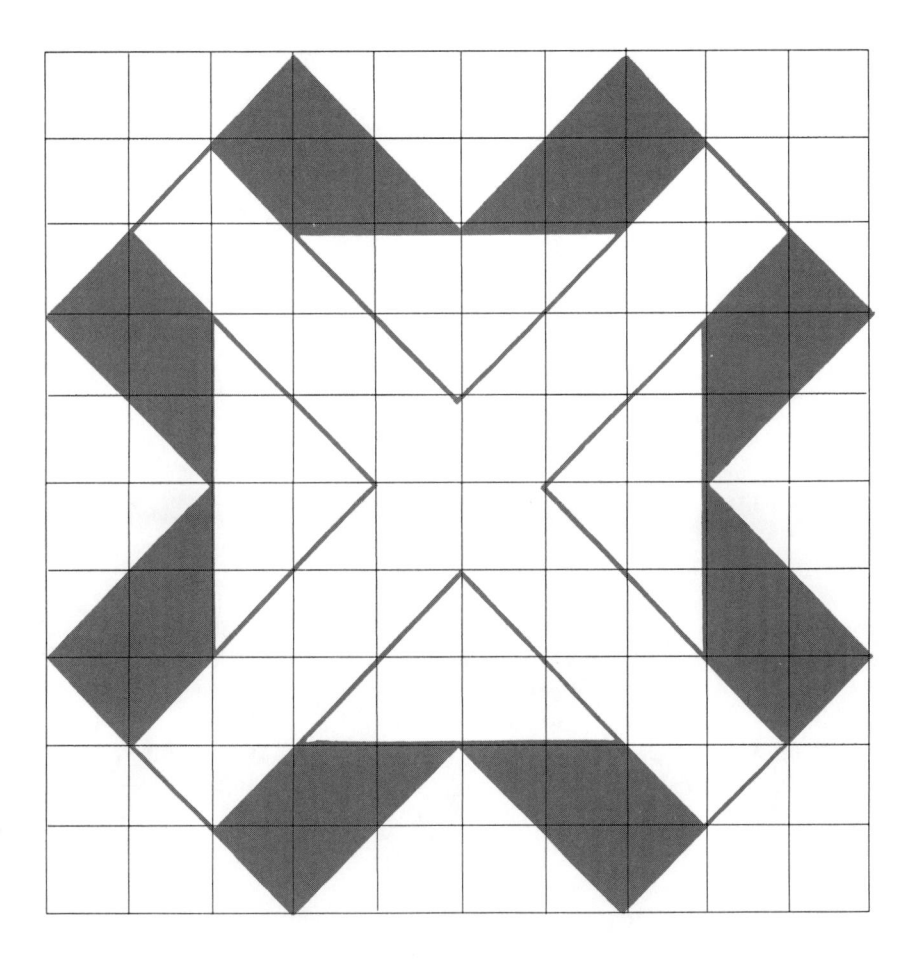

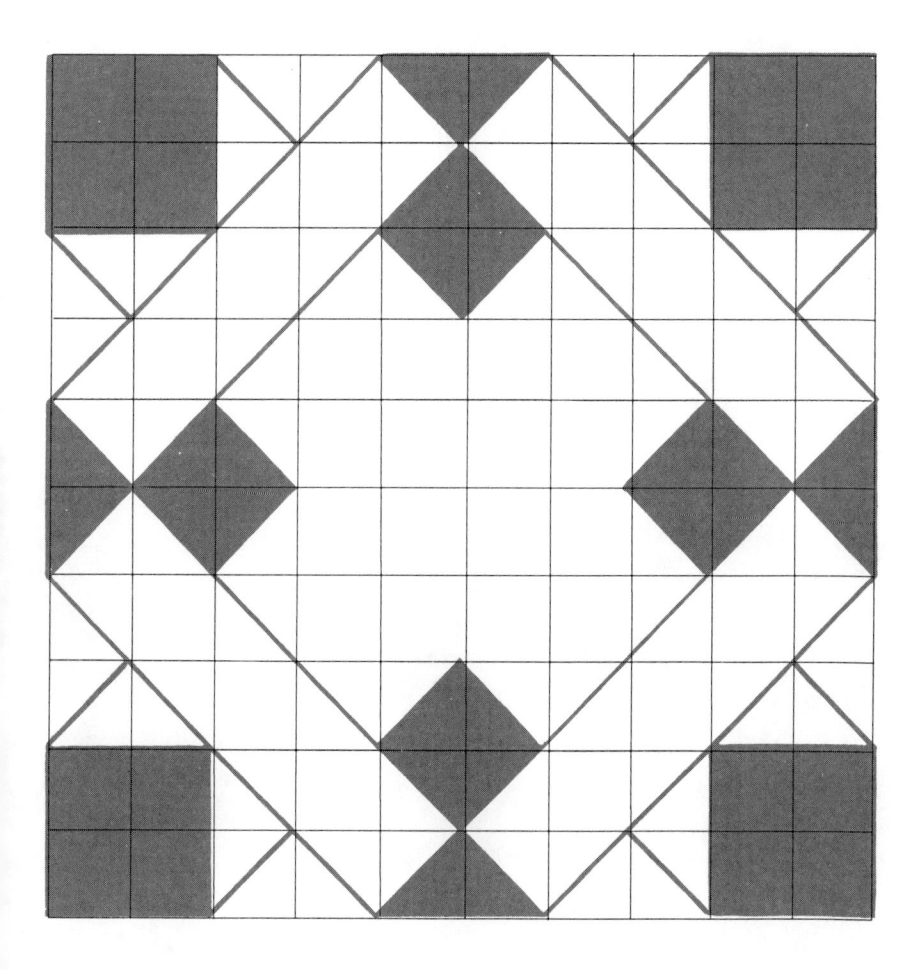

The New Testament:
Roman Cross

The New Testament:
Crowned Cross

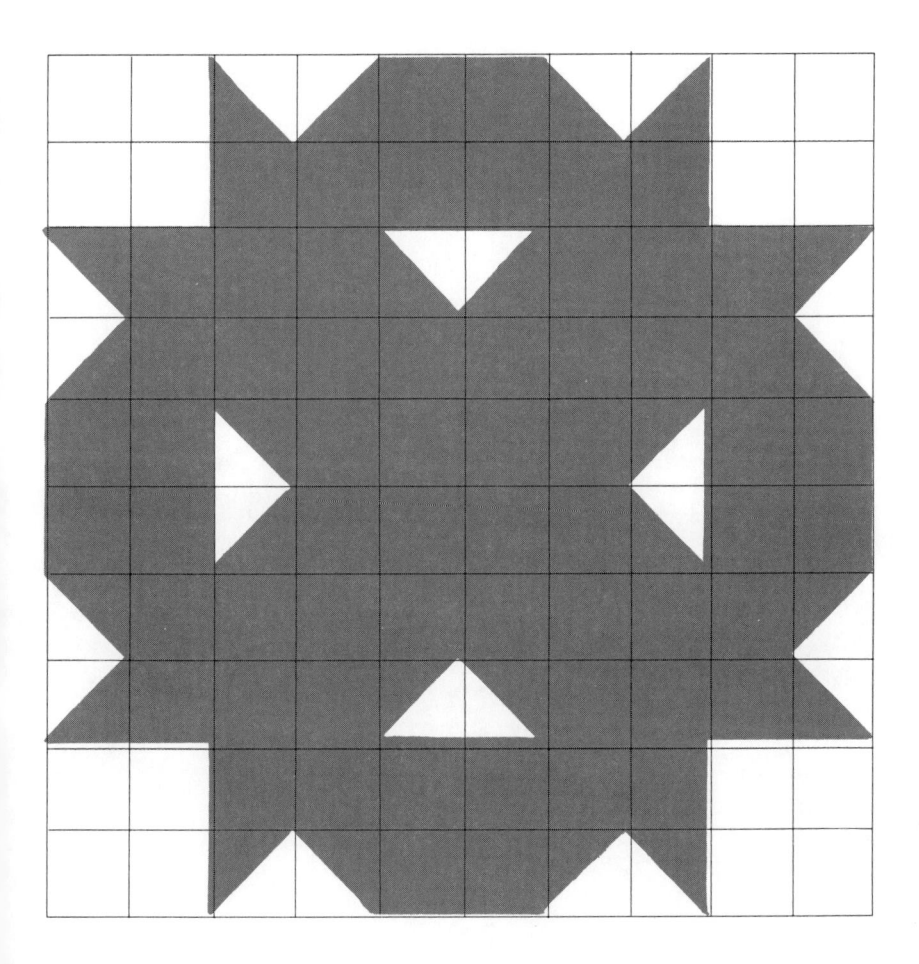

The New Testament:
Starry Crown

The New Testament:
Steps to the Altar

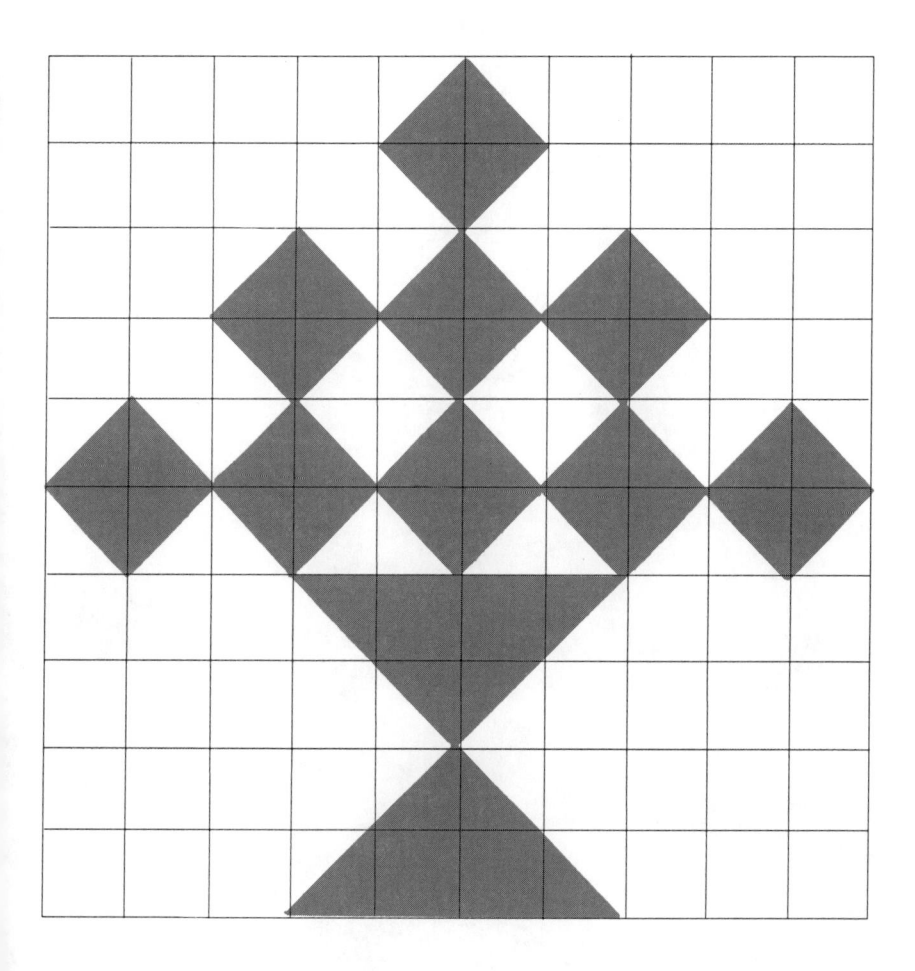

The New Testament:
The Seven Upward Steps

Faith, humility, repentance, hope, expectation, sanctification, adoption, (and on to glory).

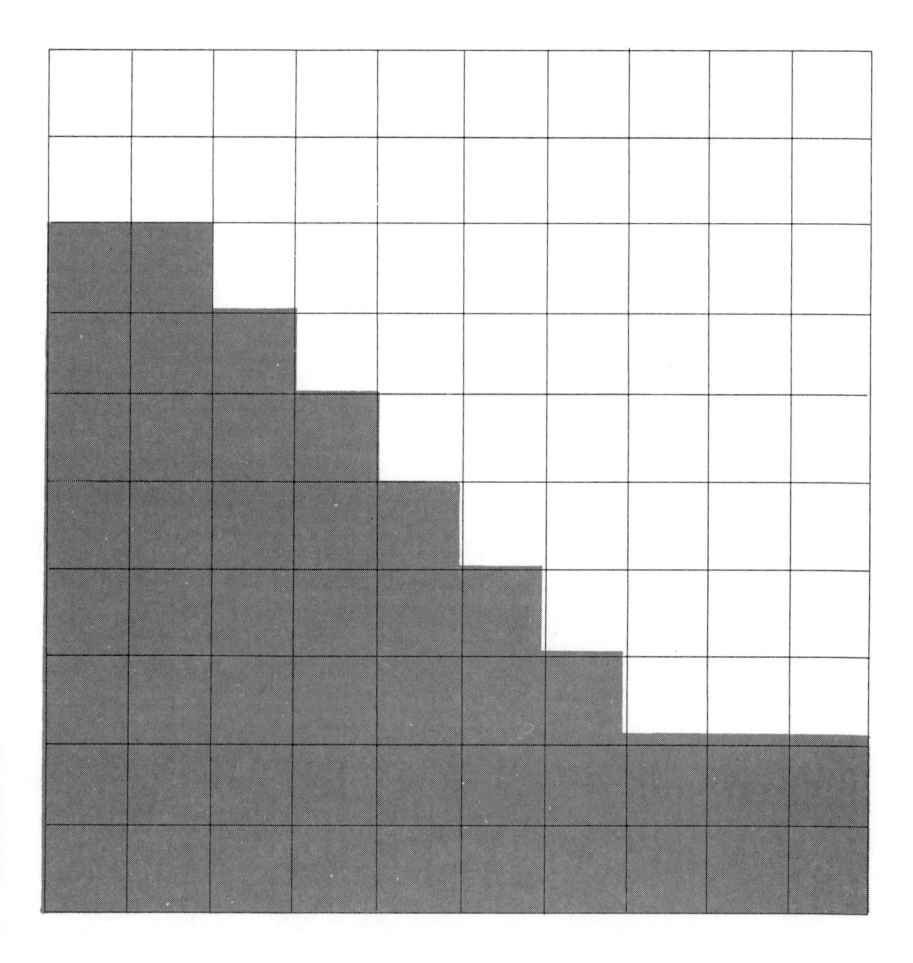

Bibliography

Bishop's Committee on Liturgy.
Environment and Art in Catholic Worship.
Washington, D.C.: USCC, 1978.

Bishop, Robert.
New Discoveries in American Quilts.
New York: E. P. Dutton & Co. Inc., 1975.

Bishop, Robert, and Elizabeth Safanda.
A Gallery of Amish Quilts.
New York: E. P. Dutton & Co. Inc., 1976.

Blair, Margot Carter.
Banners and Flags.
New York: Harcourt Brace Jovanovich, 1977.

Bradner, John.
Symbols of Church Seasons and Days.
Wilton, Conn.: Morehouse-Barlow Company, 1977.

Collopy, George.
Clip Art for Banners and Beyond.
San Jose: Resource Publications, Inc., 1988.

Collopy, George.
It's a Banner Year!
San Jose: Resource Publications, Inc., 1990.

Daves, Michael.
Young Readers Book of Christian Symbolism.
Nashville: Abingdon Press, 1967.

Ferguson, George.
Signs and Symbols in Christian Art.
New York: Oxford University Press, 1961.

Ghyka, Matila.
The Geometry of Art and Life.
Mineola, N.Y.: Dover Publications, 1978.

Gouker, Loice.
A Dictionary of Church Terms and Symbols.
Norwalk, Conn.: C. R. Gibson Co., 1974.

Ickis, Marguerite.
The Standard Book of Quilt Making and Collecting.
New York: Dover Books, 1949.

Itten, Johannes.
The Art of Color.
New York: Van Nostrand Reinhold, 1973.

Kiracofe, Roderick, and Michael Kile.
The Quilt Digest.
San Francisco: Kiracofe and Kile, 1983.

Knuth, Jill.
Banners Without Words.
San Jose: Resource Publications, Inc., 1986.

Krier, Catherine H.
Symbols for All Seasons.
San Jose: Resource Publications, Inc., 1988.

Lalibertè, Norman.
Banners and Hangings.
New York: Van Norstrand Reinhold, 1966.

Laury, Jean Ray.
Applique Stitchery.
New York: Van Nostrand Reinhold, 1966.

Matthews, Wendell.
Basic Symbols and Terms of the Church.
Philadelphia: Fortress Press, 1971.

Miles, Elaine.
Quilts and Quotes.
San Pedro: R & E Miles, 1979.

Modern Liturgy Magazine.
San Jose: Resource Publications, Inc.

Ortegel, Adelaide.
Banners and Such.
San Jose: Resource Publications, Inc.,1986.

Pavey, Donald.
Color.
Los Angeles: The Knapp Press, 1980.

Post, W. Ellwood.
Saints, Signs, and Symbols.
Wilton, Conn.: Morehouse-Barlow Company, 1962.

Rest, Friederich.
Our Christian Symbols.
Philadelphia: The Christian Education Press, 1959.

Rockland, Mae Shafter.
The Work of Our Hands.
New York: Schocken Books, 1973.

Schorsch, Anita.
Plain and Fancy.
New York: Sierling Publishing Co. Inc., 1990.

Shibukawa, Ikuyoshi, and Yumi Takahashi.
Designers' Guide to Color.
San Francisco: Chronicle Books, 1990.

_____.
Designers' Guide to Color 2.
San Francisco: Chronicle Books, 1990.

_____.
Designers' Guide to Color 3.
San Francisco: Chronicle Books, 1990.

_____.
Designers' Guide to Color 4.
San Francisco: Chronicle Books, 1990.

Sill, Gertrude Grace.
A Handbook of Symbols in Christain Art.
London: Casell & Company, Ltd., 1975.

Stockton, James.
Designer's Guide to Color.
San Francisco: Chronicle Books, 1984.

Whittemore, Carroll E.
Symbols of the Church.
Nashville: Abingdon Press, 1959.